Us, After

A Memoir
of Love
and Suicide

Rachel Zimmerman

sfwp.com

Library of Congress Cataloging-in-Publication Data

Names: Zimmerman, Rachel, 1964- author.
Title: Us, after : a memoir of love and suicide / Rachel Zimmerman.
Description: Santa Fe, NM : SFWP, [2024] | Summary: "When a state trooper appeared at Rachel Zimmerman's door to report that her husband had jumped to his death off a nearby bridge, she fell to her knees, unable to fully absorb the news. How could her husband, a devoted father and robotics professor at MIT, have committed such a violent act? How would she explain this to her young daughters? And could she have stopped him? A longtime journalist, she probed obsessively, believing answers would help her survive. She interviewed doctors, suicide researchers and a man who jumped off the same bridge and lived. Us, After examines domestic devastation and resurgence, digging into the struggle between public private selves, life's shifting perspectives, the work of motherhood, and the secrets we keep. In this memoir, Zimmerman confronts the unimaginable and discovers the good in what remains"—Provided by publisher.
Identifiers: LCCN 2023034614 (print) | LCCN 2023034615 (ebook) | ISBN 9781951631352 (trade paperback) | ISBN 9781951631369 (ebook)
Subjects: LCSH: Suicide—Biography. | Suicide—Psychological aspects. | Love—Psychological aspects.
Classification: LCC HV6545 .Z54 2024 (print) | LCC HV6545 (ebook) | DDC 362.28—dc23/eng/20231130
LC record available at https://lccn.loc.gov/2023034614
LC ebook record available at https://lccn.loc.gov/2023034615

Published by SFWP
369 Montezuma Ave. #350
Santa Fe, NM 87501
www.sfwp.com

For my daughters

At the end of my suffering
there was a door.

—Louise Glück, *The Wild Iris*

Table of Contents

Author's Note

Memoir is constructed from memories, which are, of course, subjective and fallible. The material in this book is my best effort to recollect events, including fact-checking with sources, and reviewing notes and records when available. However, I am certain others will have their own ideas about how specific scenes and actions unfolded. I take full responsibility for my version of this story. When asked, I've changed a few names and identifying features to ensure people's privacy. My children have given their consent to be included, and named, in this book.

Needless to say, the content in *Us, After* includes material that may be disturbing. If you are having thoughts of suicide, please reach out for help. Call or text 988 for the Suicide and Crisis Lifeline or go to https://www.speakingofsuicide.com/resources/ for additional resources.

Prologue

Age is a construct, my father used to say. So, despite turning 50, I slipped on a pink party dress, determined to celebrate. It was mid-March. Snow still covered the ground. My husband Seth, with only a slight nudge, had arranged a festive dinner with our favorite friends at a funky neighborhood spot. Seated at banquettes shoulder-to-shoulder, we shared confidences about our kids' first crushes and news of unexpected work coups while indulging in fava bean pâté and feta-filled gnocchi with black mission figs. Raising our flutes of sparkling rosé, we toasted to lasting connections, another year of possibilities. Seth pushed his chair back and stood. "To my beautiful wife," he said. In his eyes, I recognized a rekindling of our first glimpse of each other 15 years earlier. Laughter rose above the crowded table as we lingered, in our bubble, late into the night. It struck me that fifty was sexy and wise—not too bad.

A few months later, it was Seth turning fifty. On a balmy, late May afternoon, I sliced limes to top off pitchers of icy gin-and-tonics while keeping one eye on the kids in the yard hosing mud off one another. There were the fifth graders, friends of our 11-year-old daughter, Sophia, organizing Capture the Flag teams among the little kids, second grade classmates of our youngest, Julia, age eight. This party marked the start of summer: We blasted "Happy" by Pharrell and felt an easy flutter in our hips as we pulled our confidantes in for full-body hugs. "Happy Birthday, man," the guys said to Seth, with tenderness. That night, my husband held my face in his hands and thanked me for such a great time. "I loved it," he said. We made out in bed, and then, dulled by the mix of alcohol, food, and strong sun, began drifting off toward sleep.

"We're good," I whispered. "Fifty is okay."

"Well," he said. "It beats the alternative."

The next day, everyone emailed me, bubbling about the terrific party, how they'd felt surrounded by love. These friends couldn't have known that for many of them, it was the last time they'd ever see Seth.

PART I

Chapter 1

Widow

I f I were writing a news story, I'd start like this:

On July 1, 2014, Seth Teller, MIT professor and father of two, parked his crimson Honda Insight on the Tobin Bridge, three miles from his home in Cambridge, Massachusetts, and jumped to his death. He was 50.

But this is not that story.

This is the story of what happened after.

A grim-faced state trooper pulled up to my house. I saw him from the living room window as he stepped out of the cruiser. He slammed the car door shut and took his time letting himself in through the wooden gate. He turned down the stone path. His slow, plodding footsteps gave him away. I flung open the front door and rushed down the steps toward him.

Part of me knew before I asked.

I remember the opposing compulsions tugging me in two at that moment: I want to know, I don't want to know, like a child in a field, picking petals off a daisy. He loves me, he loves me not. I hesitated, just for a second, to speak. But the cop had a mission to complete. He was steady, stone-faced, with militaristic precision to his steps.

All morning, I'd been desperate for news of Seth, and here, finally, was the messenger. So often, the truth is nuanced, multifaceted, subjective, shaded gray. But this fact striding toward my doorstep was that rare, eminent type of truth: particular and inescapable.

"Is he dead?" I asked.

The cop's response began with a gesture of his head. I saw it start to move, slowly, up and then down. As it did, mine began to shift too, rotating to the right, to the left and back, almost like we were locked in a dance, except that his motions finally stopped, while mine grew steadily faster, overwhelming my entire body, shaking off every moment that came before.

The cop nodded, "Yes."

I fell to my knees, weeping, howling the only thoughts I could summon into words: "The girls, the girls, Oh God, the girls," like an old vinyl record stuck in a scratched groove. The trooper took my arm. The world collapsed into a sickening, hyper-real haze. I floated above my body briefly, saw myself below like a Sicilian widow in a Coppola movie. But I could not disassociate from the pain for my young daughters. Kneeling there, I felt I'd failed my key job as a mother, to protect them. As I tried to stand back up, my limbs, once solid, had now turned rubbery, unreliable. I leaned against the policeman as he led me back indoors, handing me over to a cousin who had arrived during my frantic morning search. Neighbors peered out their windows and over fences to see what the fuss was all about. I turned away.

As we entered my living room, the state trooper cleared his throat uncomfortably. He asked if my daughters' names were Sophia and Julia. I nodded. He looked straight at me: "There's a note." It was left on the dashboard of Seth's car, abandoned on the bridge.

I thought I'd vomit. "I don't want it in here," I said, swallowing hard against the intestinal churn. "I can't read it." My cousin walked with the cop back to his car where she took the single sheet of paper. She quickly folded it away, promising to keep it safe. Then she returned, placed her arms around my shoulders and begged me to breathe.

In that instant all of the previous roles I'd embodied—wife, journalist, daughter—dissolved. The clarity of my new vocation as a ferocious watchdog mother infused my entire nervous system. I felt myself lapse into a kind of madness. My reality seemed impossible to inhabit. How do I tell my children, "Daddy died." And, worse, *how* he died. They would never recover.

I sat on the couch, the last place I'd seen Seth that morning. My body was numb except for the dry matte of my tongue, thick and sour, like a bad piece of meat. Staring at the unfinished puzzle left on the floor, the one he'd worked on with the girls only hours earlier, I felt that language itself had betrayed me. Soothing words like "Marriage," "Promise," "Father" struck me now as poisonous, no longer bestowing the luxurious comforts that had tethered our lives. I had no backup to cling to, no map.

Yet I was fully aware of a deadline looming. The state trooper had delivered the news of Seth's death shortly before noon. Within about an hour, I'd snapped into a mental state that was laser-focused on solving a single problem: How to tell the girls. Now in my small office upstairs, I glanced at the old digital clock atop my wooden desk. This clock had traveled from my childhood bedroom with me to college, the West Coast and back to Cambridge, its glowing red display plain-spoken and direct. It now read 1:10pm. Camp pickup was at three. *How did a mother tell young children about their father's death*, I wondered. I desperately needed a script. As a journalist, there was one thing I understood well: how to track down an expert for guidance. I dialed a trusted work colleague and explained that I required fast help finding the right words for Sophia and Julia. "I'm on it," she said.

I stared out the window. It was a gorgeous day, hot, clear with the promise of a long summer ahead. The inconceivable pairing of beautiful weather and brutal luck began an eruption of prickly heat under my arms. "I can't fucking believe this," I muttered aloud, before placing my head down on the desk for relief from the sun's glare.

Ten minutes later, my colleague phoned back. I should stand by, she said. A psychiatrist from Massachusetts General Hospital who specialized in trauma would call me. Five minutes passed. The phone rang again. Accustomed to speaking with strangers, I immediately blurted out my dilemma as soon as Dr. Paula Rauch spoke her name. "My husband is dead. My kids don't know. What do I say?" As I sat clutching my phone, vaguely aware of the crowd of mourners gathering in the living room below, Rauch calmly walked me through the language I might use to explain the unimaginable to my children.

I should speak plainly, she said.

I could tell them their daddy had an illness in his brain. We couldn't see it, but just like cancer, it took over his body and made him die.

There was nothing any of us could have done. It was nobody's fault.

Don't lie, she advised, *but don't offer too many details.*

I nodded throughout, saying little, taking notes.

Let them know they are safe and you're not leaving, she said.

Acknowledge their pain. Reassure them you will muddle through, things will get better.

Hanging up, I exhaled for what felt like the first time all day. I always appreciated a solid plan. This prescription, in the form of her words, offered me a lifeline.

When the time came, I drove the quarter mile from my house to the children's camp and parked in the nearby lot. Thankfully, I wasn't alone in the car. I knew it was best to speak to the kids on my own, but I was also becoming aware of a dynamic I'd largely avoided in parenting thus far: requiring help. Before this moment, I had considered myself one of those older, therefore wiser, super-moms who could effortlessly go it alone. Now, I knew I wouldn't be able to drive the girls home by myself after telling them. So, there in the car with me was my 78-year-old mother, who'd broken the speed limit all the way from Cape Cod to Cambridge that morning when I called her with the news. I'd also asked Maria, the children's longtime babysitter, to join me for support.

They waited in the car as I stepped outside.

I fixed my eyes on the girls as I walked hesitantly toward them. I felt the contrast between the burdensome weight of my knowledge and their easy, light-hearted ignorance. I pulled out my phone and snapped a photo of Julia, cross-legged on the ground, sitting in a circle of friends, giggling and clapping hands with the other children awaiting pickup. I wanted a record of what I believed would be her final carefree moment.

In a robotic stupor, my body adopted the persona I'd rehearsed over the past hours. I was in full mothering mode: doing what I had to do. I waved. They approached me. I led them to a wobbly chrome table outside Anna's Taqueria, their favorite burrito place. I pulled both girls in close and told them I had very bad news.

"Girls, a terrible, terrible thing happened," I said, holding their small hands. I paused. "Daddy died." I couldn't bear the silence that I expected would follow, so I began chattering to fill the space. "It was kind of an accident, but worse," I said, grasping for phrasing that might offer some slight relief. "I don't know all the details, there's still a lot we don't understand. But it's true. And I am so, so sorry and I know it feels impossible now, but we will stay together and take care of each other and go on."

The disbelief on their faces was so stark that I felt I had to repeat myself. "He's dead."

Sophia, who looks like Seth—with her tight, dark curls and deep-set eyes—cried, "No!" and "How?"

Julia stood up on her chair: "I'm not even double digits yet," she wailed.

I still don't comprehend how the girls digested my words that day. I imagine that a part of them simply shut down. Even with their spongy young brains, they would only be able to absorb what they could understand, and this news was inconceivable. How could the most important man in their world disappear without warning? There had been no visible illness, no danger signs.

I was unable to soften this blow. All I could do was tighten my grip as I led them, dazed, to the car. We piled into the backseat and I put one arm around each girl, not wanting to let go. My mother reached around from the front passenger seat to touch them too, and began to cry. Maria drove us home. If the girls were surprised to see these women in the car, they didn't express it. We sat together in silence.

By the time we pulled into the driveway, the house had filled with family and friends in various states of distress: my journalist colleagues; my brother, who flew up from Washington; my old friend, Rachel. The news had spread. Food began arriving, along with deliverymen offering armfuls of flowers. Unfamiliar ringtones pierced the whispers and sobs. The yard and living room were so uncharacteristically crowded that for years after, Julia would become anxious whenever our house filled with people. "What happened?" she would ask at the start of any large gathering, bracing for the worst.

My dining room table was covered with chocolate babkas and fruit baskets and cheese platters, but the food was repulsive to me. I directed my attention instead to the children, who seemed oddly calm, coloring and reading with their uncles and grandmother. This scene was punctured whenever people from our various worlds appeared on the doorstep: the president of MIT; Sophia's fifth grade teacher; Ms. Gifford, the head of the lower school, who brought gift bags and a personal, handwritten note for each girl. I could see my kids perk up at the sight of a recognizable face, only to deflate again with the realization of what had brought these important figures to our home.

When sundown finally arrived, someone, mercifully, brought me an Ativan. The idea of a comatose sleep offered a glimpse of respite. I yearned to be unconscious, in darkness, completely shut down. That night, I tossed four extra pillows on to my bed. "We're sleeping together," I told the girls. It's something we never repeated, despite my offers, because it triggered flashbacks of that day. While I held them, I replayed the nightmare morning in my head: the unanswered calls to

Seth's phone, the rising dread, the cop arriving, the note. Each memory, I believed, eroded any hope for an untroubled future.

With my children's hot breath against my neck, and the time nearing 3am, I tried to blot out these thoughts. Soon, we would have to endure another day. There would be decisions for me to make. I tried to yield toward a woozy, drugged half-sleep, still checking, with each passing hour, that their small chests continued to rise and fall.

Chapter 2

Middle Age

Just months earlier, at Seth's fiftieth birthday party, I'd felt surrounded by the camaraderie and genuine warmth of friends, proud of the life we'd built together. Later, I would wonder what I'd missed, if I'd been too dismissive of his moodiness that spring, blindly blaming middle-age angst when it was something far more insidious.

I always knew that Seth was masterful at cloaking his stress, keeping it private and invisible. Sometimes I glimpsed his worry, but it never seemed the sign of an emergency. It's true that on the days leading up to his birthday, he became more preoccupied with aging. Little notes ("exercise before showering") and printouts of seven-minute workout routines appeared taped to his side of the bathroom mirror.

Fifty was a bother to him. It brought sciatica and sleep problems and an annoying ringing in the ears that forced him toward a consciousness of his body he'd escaped for so many easy years of mid-air leaps and lurches and slides on various sporting fields. "You're taking a lot of Advil," I'd say, shaking the nearly empty, family-sized bottle he carried around. "It's fine," he'd respond, aggravated by my hovering.

These tedious aches and pains undermined Seth's self-image as a laid-back dreamer. He taught classes at MIT wearing earth-toned shorts that hung low on his hips and routinely stayed up all night under the stars thinking about the Next. Big. Thing. Aging also interfered with his preferred activity: weekly Ultimate Frisbee games with a group of guys he'd been playing with for more than two decades. After a couple hours on the grass field at Danehy Park in Cambridge, they'd regroup in the empty lot behind Whole Foods. Over grilled burgers and hot dogs, they might smoke a little pot and talk as middle-aged guys often do about their kids and wives, sharing the small indignities of work, engineering feats they still dreamed might come true, and great ideas already lost, because too much time had slipped away.

Seth had initially rejected my idea of a birthday party for him. "Yours was good, but I don't want anything fancy," he said one night as I prepared for sleep while he was just revving up to start working. But early the next morning, he turned to me in bed. Surprisingly energized, he said: "How about just grilling in the front yard? A Sunday afternoon, with kids and games. I'll do all the set up."

My immediate reaction, as it often was to Seth's home-spun ideas, leaned lukewarm. I knew I'd end up handling most of the work while also managing the chaos of so many children loose at the house. But before I said a word, Seth jumped up, grabbed a book of 19th century children's games, and started rambling about organizing a scavenger hunt or a massive four-square competition. It had become a given in our marriage that Seth gravitated toward packs of kids, while I preferred the more discreet company of adults. Maybe this was because I hoped to forget my chaotic '70s childhood of broken bonds and allegiances, while he never wished to part from the nostalgia of his family nest. Games opened that door, it seemed. I saw his mood elevate exponentially with each new contest he conjured up. So, I quieted my inner critic, donned a good wife mantle, and tried to focus on the abundance in our lives. "That sounds great, honey," I said, rising from the sheets. "Let's do the Evite now."

It was unseasonably warm that day. Our guests were flushed and thirsty as they arrived at our East Cambridge home, the one Seth bought when he was first hired as an assistant professor. He was drawn to the neighborhood's lack of pretension, its triple-deckers and Portuguese immigrants, even the lore of a rough past (we'd heard rumors of a murder at a long-shuttered biker bar down the street). He also loved the Italian neighbors, who grew grapes for their homemade wine and delivered delicate anise pizzelle to our door at Christmas time. With a tipsy little apple tree out front, Seth felt comfortable here. It was the flip side of toney, manicured West Cambridge, with its Harvard pedigree, across town. I had moved here from my bohemian, light-drenched apartment atop a historic brownstone in Brooklyn Heights to be with Seth, leaving New York just in time to get married and settle in before the birth of our first child.

Back then, I knew no one else in town. But as our children began preschool, we made fast friends with their classmates' parents, all couples who'd had kids in their late 30s, after establishing careers and credentials. Our worlds knit together. We called on each other instinctively for advice about doulas and teachers, doctor recommendations, babysitters and the best bars for mojitos when we could manage a date night.

On the surface, we'd made it: careers established, children thriving, community.

What had I missed?

This question became my obsession.

Chapter 3

Hiding

It would take years of revisiting Seth's actions, reviewing certain patterns, to even begin grasping the extent of his emotional hiding. You could ask anyone, and they'd say Seth always appeared comfortable in his body, a strong, square-shouldered, physical guy who kissed friends, and tossed small children up into the air, catching them expertly. Even his voice had an ease to it, deep and a little scratchy, the texture of soft sand, like he'd just woken up, revitalized after a deliciously long sleep. I loved the breadth of him: An easy generosity matched with a voracious mind able to break down complexity into small bits and then rebuild the parts into something fresh and new, better than before.

Yet Seth also lived in a stew of stress and ambition. As a leading robotics professor at the highest-ranking research university in the world, he was hard-driving and strove to be the best. This described pretty much everyone at MIT, but to me, having grown up in the far less cutthroat milieu of humanities professors, Seth's relentless striving came as a surprise. I remember a casual dinner party with faculty one spring evening when all of the men jockeyed to show their importance. "How's the research?" appeared to be an innocent question, except here. These men did not dwell on the pressure of their environment—they didn't have to.

The intensity of the landscape manifested itself openly. During a 14-month period between 2014 and 2015, MIT experienced a spate of self-inflicted deaths: six students and one professor—my husband—died by suicide. In acknowledging that it had one of the highest suicide rates of any university in the country, MIT underwent a reckoning, of sorts, trying to bolster its mental health services and encourage those suffering to reach out. Stickers with the words: "It's okay to ask for help. MIT cares about mental health" were distributed to faculty members, who were encouraged to place them on their office doors. But as one undergraduate student wrote in his thesis at the time, suicide is never simply an anomalous incident at MIT—it's ambient, part of an ongoing dialogue. Suicide, he wrote, is "in the air."

Seth felt the demands of his work at all times. He was renowned in his field, but I believed he'd achieved a kind of balance because he also cared deeply about teaching and the lives of his students. He visited them in the hospital when they were sick. He invited them for supper to meet our children. He was driven to improve people's daily lives through practical engineering fixes: self-driving cars and smart wheelchairs and wearable devices to help blind people navigate dense cities. In that sense, he was so different than my own father, a philosophy professor who dealt in abstractions and pondered knotty, theoretical questions about Truth and Beauty.

Whenever Seth couldn't figure something out and his irritation escalated to anger (this might happen when printed directions were imprecise, for example, or when a new appliance failed), he'd blame the irrationality of the world. "This makes no *sense*," he would say. As if "sense" were clear and true like a red light at a small-town intersection: obvious, self-contained, indisputable.

Sometimes, I thought, he took his work too seriously. But I didn't fret about it much at the time. He was also skilled at compartmentalizing, pivoting easily, it seemed, from immersive problem-solving to a kind of frisky charm. His delight in play was apparent whether it was a beanbag toss at the local street fair or splaying out on the floor, surrounded by a 1000-piece puzzle of a fairy kingdom. "C'mon," he'd call out to the girls. "Find the edges first." His computer housed scores of video clips of the kids as toddlers, singing in the bath or jumping on our bed, Seth off camera goading them to jumble the lyrics into silly nonsense or jump even higher.

While some parents played with their kids only when summoned, with Seth it was the reverse: he was always the one to initiate a game. He spent so much time in the children's classrooms on the days he dropped them off at school that a parent once asked me if he had a "real" job.

Seth took his job as a dad to heart. While MIT is generally seen as a sober and storied beacon of academia, Seth viewed it as a playground. He'd sometimes rouse the girls on a Sunday afternoon and lead them on a circuit of fun. They'd bike over to the campus in Cambridge's Kendall Square to check in on Atlas, the hulking humanoid robot he was building with his students. Seth would let the girls test out the controls, together imagining all that this gleaming, God-like robot whose namesake held up the heavens might someday accomplish.

They'd make a pit stop at Seth's corner office on the third floor of Stata, the famously quirky Frank Gehry building adorned with off-kilter, swervy outcroppings made of mirror-surface steel, aluminum, and corrugated metal. Sophia and Julia would draw stick figures on his whiteboard or sort through boxes filled with random hardware and defunct metal parts. After that, they would burst through the glass doors out back, scrambling to the top of Mark DiSuvero's red steel structure, Aesop's Fables II. Julia had been a climber since birth, always eyeing furniture and neighborhood trees, mapping out a route to the top. Seth encouraged this even though I'd grow worried seeing her little body high up on a branch of questionable sturdiness. Their final stop on the campus tour was the basement vending machines for Good Humor Strawberry Shortcake ice cream bars, all the sweeter because they violated my no-dessert-before-dinner rule.

Seth's relationship with our daughters was central to his identity. "You are my bright star," he'd tell each girl, tucking them into bed. He'd made them believe they were safe, that he could fix anything, that they would wake up each morning to the sound of his voice.

Chapter 4

Remain Upright

I looked out over a lush hill of graves at Mount Auburn Cemetery, dehydrated, dizzy, incredulous. My head pounded as I walked toward the burial in 90-degree heat, wobbly in heels on uneven ground. In an off-balance instant, I thought, *It's just like my wedding*, when my stilettos dug into a carpet remnant set on sand. This time, though, I wore black, not white, and the scorching sun was oppressive. I smelled my own acrid sweat as I leaned against my brother to keep from falling. Parched, and with the acidity of the morning's black coffee snaking down my gut, my body no longer felt like mine to control. How could this be happening?

Two large men from the Cambridgeside Funeral Home lowered my husband's pine casket into the ground. In that moment, I felt certain I'd made the right decision leaving the children at home to skip the morning burial. These kids will have plenty of bad dreams, I thought. They didn't need to add this dark image to the ones I expected would someday take shape in their minds: the fall from the bridge, the thud of his body, the word "suicide."

The previous night, the girls had drawn rainbows on the card we'd planned to bury with Seth. There was also a family photo of the four of us with his parents, as well as another artifact: his favorite sunshine yellow T-shirt with the word "Antiphony" written across the top in black script. This was the family opera the girls and I performed in, with Sophia starring as a singing grasshopper and Julia as a tiny, rebellious ant. Just one year earlier they'd shined in the show; now the memory made me wince.

* * *

I'd rejected many of the norms and rituals that provide a blueprint for death. Despite being Jewish, we had no shiva, the tradition of receiving mourners at home. I was raised by parents who rebelled against their immigrant upbringing. This included a wholesale rejection of any devotion to Judaism. With their Socialist leanings, my parents viewed belief in organized religion as not only unnecessary, but potentially dangerous, "the opium of the people." I didn't enter a synagogue until adulthood, was unschooled in the Jewish practices surrounding the dead. Part of me was glad for this. I wanted the option of keeping the mourners out, of simply closing the door and holding my children. I didn't want the pressure of casseroles or questions. My idea of a shiva allowed for curling up on our couch together, popcorn in a bowl, with yet another episode of Gilmore Girls; escaping through the TV antics of a groovy single mom and her whip-smart daughter, navigating their rollercoaster lives in a fictional New England town.

I longed to reside in these distractions. But I had realities to face.

Seth's body, for instance. I'd chosen not to view it one last time. His cousin, a cop, who'd identified him the day he died, had warned me against it, shaking his head emphatically. "Believe me," he said. "You don't want to see him." I complied, because, no, I did not want to view my husband bruised and broken.

The casket descended, and with it, a bitter taste of loss rose up my throat. Seth died on the first day of the month and was buried on the sixth, a Sunday, the end of Independence Day weekend.

Most years on the Fourth of July, we headed to the town parade in Wellfleet on Cape Cod. Seth would set lawn chairs up on the sidelines and we'd watch the show: kids dressed as lobsters, wizened men driving antique roadsters, and ladies from the Chamber of Commerce tossing candy and bubblegum and cheap sparkly necklaces in red, blue, and gold as they passed.

As I thought of this, I felt ashamed. I knew my husband, slept next to him for 15 years, scratched his back at night. We knew each other: He shot video of me giving birth to our children. How could I, a professional observer, miss the main story, not even pick up the hints?

People who study suicide talk about a kind of tunnel vision that envelops a person who has decided to end his life. But how could Seth's view narrow so much that it no longer captured our girls? Were we somehow not enough?

Sophia asked a question on the day of Seth's death, and it stuck in my mind: "Will we ever be happy again?" I said yes, but didn't believe it. We were shattered, irreparably so, I was sure. From the moment Seth died, all I wanted to do was shield the girls. Their childhoods had been cut short and I felt it was now on me to become a kind of relentless archeologist, to help them extract microscopic bits of pleasure buried deep in the earth. That meant digging up traces of good in the aftermath of disaster. I had no clue how to do that, but I steadied myself, trying to remain upright, fighting the urge to collapse into a heap on the ground.

As their father was buried, the girls read stories with their cousins at home, and noshed on the gift-wrapped chocolates and rugelach that kept arriving by mail. This would not erase any heartache, of course, but baked goods from Zabar's might offer a fleeting consolation before they had to climb upstairs to their rooms to choose black dresses and hairdos for the memorial service later that day.

I nearly canceled the service at the last minute due to my turmoil over what to wear. Nothing was right. My friend Kira had rushed over to help. She pulled a form-fitting purple dress with psychedelic swirls off its hanger. "Purple is a traditional mourning color," she assured me.

But for a suicide? Purple was too giddy. I did want to look intact, to assuage the fears of my guests and my children, and channel a kind of reassurance that I wouldn't break down. But I also wanted my appearance to reflect appropriate despair. I yanked free the sleeveless gray-and-black striped dress I'd bought at a Provincetown boutique and held it up to my body. This one felt better: just enough grieving widow, but also with a tinge of levity. It hugged my five-foot frame and, I believed, would project the illusion of being pulled together.

When it was time, I drove with my mother and children the short distance to the MIT Chapel—a brick-covered cylindrical sanctuary in the middle of campus surrounded by a gentle reflecting moat. Years before, Seth and I had wandered in after a date and kissed in the stained-glass entryway, the cool moonlight upon us. Now the harsh light of midday filled the vestibule.

I stood in my striped dress at the front of the chapel, greeting guests as they arrived. The summer heat brought a sense of intimacy; this ritual of gathering together awakened long-dormant relationships. Here's my high-school dance teacher who'd changed her name to Penelope Cake; a loyal ex-boyfriend from Portland; the bad boss no one had invited; my divorced parents, rarely in the same room together; the massage therapist who'd worked on Seth the day before he died and wondered about her culpability; my ob-gyn, who'd taught Seth balancing-spoon tricks while I was in labor; and all the girls' teachers. And Mrs. Dello Russo, who told me Julia would be in her third grade class in the fall, and that she'd take care of her. Seth's parents, ashen and aged, held out their arms to me, without the words to speak. What could they say, after all, they'd lost their youngest son.

Relatives offered—begged, really—to bring me food. My gut in a knot, I was down to a child's weight. My mother dug into her purse and pulled out a little piece of muffin wrapped in a napkin. One of Seth's aunts held out a yogurt as an offering. Friends and family cried at the sight of me with my girls. I buried my face in their necks: "Can you fucking believe this?" I said to my closest girlfriends, and, "No, mom, I don't want a muffin."

I was desperate to gain control over my life in any way possible. "You sit there," I commanded the guests. "No video allowed." I shut down all questions about how or why he died. I silenced any talk of bridges or heights in front of the children. I'd been a journalist for over 20 years, but wanted no in-depth reporting of my sorrow, no speculation or inquiry about how my daughters' lives had been hijacked.

The chapel was packed, so we ushered all the children—friends and classmates of the girls—to the low steps below the altar. They faced outward toward the sanctuary and formed a tableau of big-eyed, flush-faced, stricken beauties. Some of the sad, confused girls awkwardly draped their bare arms around each other, unsure how they were supposed to behave.

Mourners sat fanning themselves with their programs, which had pictures of Seth printed across the page. With each motion, his face appeared and disappeared: an image of him on a beach in Italy cropped to show his robust chest hair; a close-up of his face, serious and intense, directing Atlas, the robot; Seth posed in a rare moment, dressed-up in a dark suit and lavender shirt, a Sears portrait for his parents; and finally, that recognizable profile, chiseled and handsome, grinning broadly and wearing a black wool cap.

In all of the photos he beamed irrepressibly. Everyone knew that smile. It cloaked him in an easy radiance. Speaker after speaker described Seth's big dreaming. How he'd stay up all night to watch a meteor shower with his cousins while they plotted fixes to hard problems—like how to clear radioactive waste from a nuclear disaster site using robots—the kinds of ideas that put him on the cusp of fame in his field. Friends spoke of his earthy, kid-centric side and insistence on wearing shorts to every occasion. (He'd won a bet in graduate school—no long pants for an entire year—and the habit stuck.)

I listened, marveling at how cool my husband had been. I was always proud to walk into a room with him, with that brain and that grin. In the end, that's what this gathering was for, to remind the children that their father was a hero right up until the moment of his death. We pictured the sweet man who'd organized family reunions, called his male cousins "baby," and reached for my hand every time the plane took off.

Though I was faint and nauseous, I stood to speak. I wanted my daughters to see me rise up proudly in front of all our people, to hear me testify that their dad was the love of my life and that they were his dream. I believed they needed to be lifted by the story of our marriage. I spoke about how he'd waited until he had tenure before proposing to ensure professional and financial security. On that overcast April day, we drove out to the dunes at Newcomb Hollow in Wellfleet. There, he'd unveiled an antique ring and a split of champagne.

I offered stories to illustrate his love. After Sophia was born, on my very first Mother's Day, Seth wrote me a note: "Thank you for taking such good care of me, Mommy." He'd dipped her tiny, two-month-old feet in pink and blue ink and pressed them onto the page.

I tried to paint a beautiful picture for the children, so the father they remembered wouldn't slip away: Seth rocking them to sleep, singing "You Are My Sunshine," reciting the rules of Ultimate Frisbee when they were infants. I told them about the many ways they were like him. I saw him in Julia's wise observations. As a five-year-old, sitting in the car with her seatbelt stuck and broken, Julia shook her head and muttered, "design flaw," a favorite phrase of her father's.

When Sophia was in fourth grade, Seth took her to the MIT field and taught her how to long jump in preparation for her school's Greek Olympics. He handed down his love of the ancient myths; often they'd sit together quietly, each with a book. Somehow, they could shut out the world.

Up there at the altar, with the fervor of purpose, I recited Mary Oliver as I had at our wedding, a different part of the same poem:

"I don't want to end up simply having visited this world." I leaned forward on my toes, and looked at each of my daughters directly: "Your Daddy, in his short time, changed the world. He had big ideas and a big heart, and you have those things, too, because he will always be a part of you."

Then Julia rose to sing.

My younger daughter climbed up the steps by herself, eight years old, petite except for the halo of irrepressible caramel brown curls framing her face. She wore a black-and-white A-line dress that reminded me of the oversized half-moon cookies, iced vanilla and chocolate, that my mother used to buy for us at the neighborhood bakery. Watching her approach the microphone, I heard gasps from the audience. My throat tightened too. Until that moment, I'd been stoically in control. But when I saw my brave daughter up there with nothing more than her favorite Adele song, my heart split open with regret for what she'd lost.

"Never mind I'll find someone like you." She sang with a voice so big the whole room stilled. The song seemed to grow from deep inside her, as if she were breathing Seth in, pulling him toward her by force of will. She was conjuring him—her sweet dad gone, but present, somehow, in the center of her body, in her breath. I listened to the words:

> *"Don't forget me, I beg. I'll remember, you said.*
> *Sometimes it lasts in love and sometimes it hurts instead."*

All at once, I felt alone. I was this little girl's sole protector, with no script, just a wish. Make it better, make me strong. And a question: *How can we go on?*

Chapter 5

The Equivalence of Loss

That first summer after Seth's death, there were bank accounts, mortgages, car payments, and growing stacks of legal documents that required my attention. We were fortunate in that our finances were stable. But this wasn't immediately apparent, not to me. I worried that without Seth's income I'd have to upend my kids' world, move to a smaller place, remove them from their familiar school, cancel the various activities that grounded them. He'd secured a generous life insurance policy through work, but I was left in limbo, waiting to learn if it would be honored in the case of a suicide. I'd have to negotiate our health insurance, social security payments, and the other benefits we received through Seth. Months later, when I got word that most of these benefits would remain intact, I realized the centrality of this support: we could continue our routines and sustain our lives mostly as they were.

Yet at the time I didn't feel as lucky as I was. I panicked realizing all our financial documents were in his name. Somehow, over time, we'd slipped into the gendered roles of a traditional marriage where Seth took care of the money and I dealt with the children. It would take me years to sort everything out. Topping the list of immediate obstacles was Bank of America, whose corporate officers somehow believed that I was the one who'd died, and promptly froze all of our accounts. They sent Seth a letter expressing their sincere condolences on the death of his spouse.

Groggy from the emotional burden of paperwork, I'd struggle to get through the days: completing a single task was an accomplishment. Maria, who I began to think of as "our" babysitter because of the many ways she cared for me as well as the children, would play cards with them for hours, or take them to the neighborhood playground while I dealt with the accounts. She graciously offered to handle tasks I couldn't face, like clearing Seth's toiletries from the bathroom. I could live without those, but I fretted over what to do with his clothes: the soft cotton shirts that dominated his wardrobe, the suit he wore on our wedding day. I couldn't throw them away, but I couldn't look at them either. In the end, Maria stuffed dozens of T-shirts, shorts, and jeans into garbage bags and dragged them down to the basement.

This early period of unrelenting physical and psychic unease was centered in the middle of my chest, a perpetual brick-like weight pressing against my heart. I couldn't shake the fact that I'd failed to protect my kids. This thought kept circling around me, buzzing nonstop like a kamikaze gnat, leaving me unable to focus. Those first weeks and months, I was just a zombie girl, stumbling through each hour of every day, from breakfast to dinner to sleep.

I took a leave from my job at the Boston public radio station. With the funeral over and critical papers signed, I somehow funneled the three of us into the car. We escaped to my mother's cottage in Wellfleet, a couple of hours away.

My parents had bought the grey-shingled cottage on a hill and an acre of land the year I was born. Every time the house came into view, I entered a world saturated in vivid memories: my father's arms around me as we danced to Donovan's "Mellow Yellow" on the phonograph, waiting for the shower after a day at the beach; see-sawing with my little brother on the rusty jungle gym; watching my dad drive away in a butter yellow VW bug—the moment that, for me, marked the end of their marriage.

As kids, my brother and I spent every summer in Wellfleet. Back then, it was still a sleepy beach town that attracted artists and intellectuals. For us, coming from Brooklyn, the Cape was the closest thing to small-town America we'd ever known. There was a party line on our telephone, and we only had to dial 9 and then a four-digit exchange to reach our neighbors. Sometimes, one of those neighbors, a boy my age, would meet me at a hidden, unclaimed plot, where we'd lay in the tall grass and play doctor. He'd place little pieces of paper inside me and call them prescriptions.

In the '70s, there were no tchotchke shops lining the one-street town, no racks of sun hats or oyster tank tops on display. Rather, a single breakfast spot anchored the place. It was called The Lighthouse, and on rare mornings we'd eat out, ordering warm blueberry muffins topped with thick slabs of melting butter. Next door, The Penny Patch, with sawdust on its wood-plank floors, offered the most wonderful assortment of sweets: candy necklaces, chocolate-filled "cigarettes," and rolls of cash register paper lined with hard-shelled sugar-dots in yellow, pink, and blue.

Our Wellfleet traditions spanned decades, but after my parents' divorce, the arrangements shifted slightly. My mother would stay with us in July and then return to Brooklyn just as my father and stepmother arrived for the month of August. The adults believed this arrangement provided stability, and it did offer the illusion of a seamless summer. After all, we slept each night in the same rooms, our single beds covered with soft, Winnie-the-Pooh sheets and matching pillowcases.

But Mom's July was like living on another planet compared to Dad's August. July meant structure and predictability: carob bars and fruit rolls after Red Cross swimming lessons every morning at Gull Pond. We'd spend long afternoons at the ocean, the mothers sitting in beach chairs and the kids sprawled on towels nearby. After supper, we'd pile back into the car barefoot and order soft serve from PJ's, our cones dipped in chocolate that would harden into a dark casing before our eyes.

On special nights, we'd bundle up in pajamas, throw pillows in the back of the car and head to the drive-in, where we'd jump onto the playground's spinning, metal whirlybird—my brother called it "The Wheel of Death"—until the sky darkened and the previews began.

In August, those routines evaporated. During the day, we'd swim at Great Pond, where we first met the woman who would become our stepmother, an English literature major and former student of Dad's. At 5pm she'd mix drinks for everyone, scotch or gin for them, Coke with a splash of Vermouth for us. Some nights, my father took us to beach parties where there was talk of politics and war. The men held cans of Rheingold. We'd fall asleep on the drive home and Dad would carry us into bed from the car.

* * *

As I maneuvered my car up the hill to the Wellfleet cottage, I spotted my mother's familiar figure waving. I already sensed her anxiety as she stood in the doorway wearing her faded jeans, grey hair in girlish braids, and a dish towel thrown over her shoulder, having just washed and cut up a melon in preparation for the girls' arrival. She approached the car before I even turned off the engine, and I realized both the comfort of her presence and, also, my dread. I began unloading the bags, but I could barely speak, despite my mother's solicitousness. She embodied my deepest fear: a single mom raising two kids alone. I can't become her, I thought, but I was nearly there.

My mother, particularly in those first years after her divorce, was erratic. More than once, when we balked at leaving the pond at the designated time, she'd threaten us: "I'm getting in the car and driving away." We were pretty sure she'd come back, and she always did. But as we stood on the grass at Long Pond shivering, clutching out towels, we were never certain.

Other times, when we worked up the nerve to ask Mom for a favor, like giving one of the other summer kids a ride home, she'd explode. "That kid has two parents," she'd scream. "Why doesn't one of their parents drive them?" A common refrain of hers was, "How *dare* you?"

My brother, who would later become a lawyer, and who always knew how to weaponize an argument when needed, tried to reason with her. One night, their yelling grew so loud it hurt my ears, and I hid in my bed staring at the black pine knots in the walls until they turned into big-eyed ghouls. I heard a ceramic lamp shatter and saw through the slit under my door that the living room had gone dark.

My mother was blindsided by her husband's affair. I now understand that the extreme betrayal she experienced when my father left caused her grief to transform into a toxic anger. We were three and five when he moved out, and suddenly, my mother lost her naive innocence. She'd always believed people did what they said. She could not imagine the situation she found herself in: on her own with small children, abandoned by a man who'd vowed to love and protect her.

Over the years, she took on the guise of a survivor, developing a hard edge. She never remarried. She told me that, when my brother and I would leave on Friday nights to spend the weekend at my dad's, she'd remain in bed, depressed until we returned on Sunday morning. Then she'd trudge off to work early Monday, to a public high school in Greenpoint where she taught English. Her fragility meant that small trespasses derailed her. She took me for a haircut once in the dead of winter. The stylist was late, and then, as she began cutting, made some flippant comment about tardiness and my mother erupted. "That's it," she said, her patience snapped. She dragged me out of the salon with my hair wet, my new shag cut only half completed. By the time we got home, my long, uneven bangs were frozen in place.

One Friday night when I was in high school, I hurriedly packed a bag to take to my father's, a short, four-block walk from my mother's apartment. I'd left my room a mess, thus violating the rule that we straighten up our bedrooms before departing for the weekend. When

I returned Sunday morning, I opened my door. All my belongings—clothes, the contents of my desk and closet—formed a heap in the middle of the room. I recoiled in shock and turned. My mother stood glaring behind me.

"Now you know how it feels to live with a mess," she yelled.

"You're crazy," I screamed.

Distraught, needing to escape, I rushed past her without even stopping to put on shoes. I ran out of the apartment barefoot and found a stoop around the corner where I sat and sobbed.

Though my mother did have a few long, loving relationships over the years, she kept her boyfriends at a distance, perhaps trying to reassure us of our primacy in her life. None of them ever slept over when we were home. I don't recall sharing a single meal together. She still lives alone in the same two-bedroom apartment where I grew up. Many years later, I'd note the hallmarks of solitary living: food half eaten and uncovered in the refrigerator; no attention paid to doors that don't fully close, having been painted and repainted so many times over decades. I vowed that would never be me.

* * *

My mother tried her best to help us during the two months we stayed with her after Seth died. She cooked the girls soft scrambled eggs and sweet potatoes for supper and took them to the public library on days I couldn't get out of bed. She offered me meals, too, and book suggestions, and rides to the pond. I said no often. Helping me was nearly impossible. There was no comfort food, no comfort at all. I couldn't concentrate long enough to read a magazine, let alone lose myself in the pleasure of a book. During the day, I'd walk from the house down the hill out of ear shot, and call experts for advice on how to talk about suicide with the children or whether I should force them to go to therapy. I vacillated between anger toward Seth for leaving us—for abandoning me—and extreme sorrow over what he must have been feeling to commit such a violent act. I was desperate for guidance, believing I'd lost the ability to trust my instincts.

One early morning, as I dragged myself into the kitchen for coffee, my mother said she'd been thinking. Gently, she suggested that she understood what it was like for me as a newly single mom, since she, too, had been left to raise two kids. Standing there in her little white nightgown, still with the dish towel over her shoulder, she said: "I was abandoned, too."

This equivalence enraged me. "Really?" I snarled. "You're comparing divorce to death? You had every weekend free, we had a father to go to." Despite my parents' chilly relationship, they would call on each other whenever there was an accident or an emergency. "I have no one," I said, grabbing my black coffee and storming off. I was my own contingency plan, and that idea was perhaps the most terrifying of all.

But my mother didn't let go. And each time she tried to show understanding or reach out with a knowing gesture of sisterhood-in-grief, I was repulsed. All I could hear was her distorted symmetry, equating her divorce with my widowhood. With every show of kindness, I grew more enraged. "Death is not the same as divorce!" I would scream, rushing to my bedroom at the back of the house, slamming the door.

"Rachel, I'm sorry," she would say. I could tell she meant it. But I'd only dig in deeper and let my despair seethe: "Their father is DEAD," I yelled, so loud my throat hurt. "How *dare* you?"

What made matters worse is that I actually understood her logic. Our circumstances did match up. We were, in fact, both single mothers, not by choice. We were angry and anxious, channeling our losses into the fierce protection of our children. But where I'd once seen her turbulent behavior as a personality flaw, I now understood it to be a result of her abandonment. She experienced their divorce as a kind of death. Many years later, she told me about her long nights alone, eating entire Entenmann's cakes with her hands. I had no idea then how she'd suffered. How she, too, felt she'd lost control of her life. And how she'd tried to snatch it back in ineffective ways. This may be why she was always on some kind of diet when I was growing up, and why I joined her in rigid calorie-counting for years and then decades: half a grapefruit and toast all day, scooping out the carb guts of a bagel, our refrigerator full of nonfat cottage cheese and sugar-free ice milk—none of it with any taste.

Now, along with our shared, interminable desire to lose 10 more pounds, my mother and I were linked in another way: we'd been betrayed by the men who claimed they'd remain.

That first summer, I allowed my bitterness to go rogue and unfettered. I stewed about the sheer injustice of my plight, vacillating between anguish over my fractured little family, and a penetrating, full-body numbness. When Robin Williams died by suicide shortly after Seth, I received several notes asking if I was okay. I trashed those messages, resenting that I'd somehow become the go-to guy for all suicide-related news. I did respond to one person, though, in the inappropriate, unfiltered manner I'd adopted: "At least no one hanged themselves in my house."

I took Ativan every night to sleep. Even so, scenes from the day Seth died replayed in a loop: that morning, when I returned to our house and his car was gone; the frantic calls to friends, family, and finally, 911; the unanswered texts, and then, finding his phone under the pillow in our bed. Perhaps he didn't want my voice to interfere with his plan, nor my recurring messages that might have made him reconsider. The final text I sent Seth still lives with me, embedded, like a virus, ready to flare when my guard is down. Every time I replace my cell phone, for instance, there's a spike of dread awaiting the transfer of old texts. "Are you sure they'll all be saved?" I ask the AT&T technician. "Yeah," he says, confused by my urgency. "Are you absolutely sure?" I repeat. Then I stand still, not budging from the counter until I see that text dated July 1, 2014, appear on the screen: "Please call me ASAP. I love you come home."

* * *

In Wellfleet, I coaxed the girls to join me for a daily swim in the ocean, no matter how cold. Sometimes we took rubber rafts and rode waves all the way to shore, a short-term thrill that punctured our lurking sadness. Other days we'd stop at one of the gem-like freshwater kettle ponds formed by melting glacial deposits more than 15,000 years before. There was Long Pond with its old wooden dock for diving, and Gull Pond with its narrow waterway, "the Sluice," on the far side that felt like our own secret cove. We'd visited these spots so many times as a family that the excursions felt almost normal, as if Seth were just away for the day, and we'd pick him up later at the Provincetown airport, where the girls would rush to him and he'd drop his bag as they jumped into his arms. Sometimes, I'd inadvertently put a fourth towel out for him on the sand.

That summer, the low tides seemed especially low. At the Bay, we'd walk out for nearly a quarter mile, our bare feet side-stepping horseshoe crabs and barnacled razor clams, entire neighborhoods of sea life. At sunset, we'd marvel at the view across the water, toward the Provincetown monument. I wondered: if Seth had seen one more of these glorious rose sunsets, if he'd watched Julia do fifty cartwheels in a row on the sand, if he'd heard Sophia sing "Unwritten" in the outdoor shower, would he, perhaps, have reconsidered? Maybe he'd have reconnected to a trove of beauty and wonder—her voice, her muscular little body—and snapped out of his descent.

But Seth wasn't one to reach for a lifeline. He rarely spoke of his problems. We were different that way. I was raised by parents who came of age experimenting with radical therapies and all manner of self-exploration. My father assembled his own "orgone-accumulator," a small, sauna-like box, but without the heat, in deference to Wilhelm Reich, the renegade psychoanalyst who believed that certain concentrated energies could be curative. My mother, especially, extolled self-expression: "Get your feelings out in the open or you'll get sick! Don't hold it in!"

There were so many feelings to contain, though, in the chaos of growing up. Suddenly, there was a woman, 15 years younger than my father, living with him. Although their relationship lasted 50 years, it seemed awfully tenuous at the start. Early on, my brother and I weren't completely sure of her role in the family. Once, during our summer stint with my dad and stepmother, we befriended a neighbor, a kind, elderly metalworker. Near the end of our stay, this neighbor surprised us with gifts: two thick bronze pendants each dangling from a strand of leather. As he handed us the necklaces, he gestured up to our rental cottage. "Is that your mother," he asked. My brother and I, then about 6 and 8, looked at each other. We paused for an instant, then I said "Yes" and he said "No" at precisely the same time.

The disequilibrium at my dad's was both exciting and precarious. In order to travel, my father would sometimes take summer teaching jobs in far-flung places. When I was 16, he brought me along to San Miguel de Allende, in Mexico, where we lived in the apartment of artist friends, atop a courtyard filled with peacocks and pools of cool water and lush greenery. When my dad ran out of pot, I watched from a window as he tried to score some weed from a local guy on the street. Dad's Spanish was non-existent, I could see him pantomiming smoking a joint, while the confused stranger just shook his head. That summer, my father climbed up onto a glass table in the apartment trying to straighten a picture on the wall. As my stepmother pleaded, "Bob, get off the table," he ignored her, reaching up further and further still until his weight caused the table to buckle and shatter. I ran downstairs to find my father laying in a pool of glass shards.

Seth was the opposite: self-contained and acutely aware of the physics of his body. He had an affable relationship with my father that stemmed from their mutual curiosity about the world, but Seth always pushed my dad to identify the true value—the fix-it quotient—of philosophy. "How does *The Phenomenology of Spirit* actually help us, Bob?" he'd ask, sitting around the living room in Brooklyn when we'd visit. "What aspect of our lives does it improve?" My dad, amused by Seth's difficulty with abstraction, would say: "Why Seth, it helps us to think."

I thought of their differences often. The kid-centric guy who built robots, and the charming intellectual, never quite clued in to the basic needs of small children, once offering my toddler daughter a stapler and a metal bust of Nietzsche to play with. They both had an intrinsic love of inquiry, though, and a compulsion to make people understand the world more clearly. For my father, this impulse took many forms. He invented logic games for long car rides. He explained, at bath time, that there was, on one hand, "the physical bar of soap," and on the other, "the *idea* of soap." During Watergate, when I was about 10, he told me, in earnest, that I could marry anyone, as long as he wasn't a Republican.

And they both adored their children. I'd tell Seth stories about growing up in Brooklyn Heights, and all the weekends my father drove us into the city to see the Paper Bag players perform political theatre, or to Madison Square Garden during the Knicks heyday, when we'd cheer for Walt and Earl and Dave DeBusschere and Bill Bradley. Heading home, we often stopped for egg creams at Dave's luncheonette on Broadway.

Later, at Sarah Lawrence, where my father taught and I was a student, we'd visit together in his small office. Surrounded by books balanced precariously on overstuffed shelves, his desk covered in burn marks from cigarettes left unattended, we'd talk about ideas for our writing. This was when I was involved in the New York modern dance scene, and Dad and I would discuss the "isms" in art—postmodernism and deconstructivism. He loved the clean formalism of Merce Cunningham, the romantic flourishes of Douglas Dunn, and he'd find ways to weave my interests into his latest articles on aesthetic theory. I had adopted his writing style: vast, paragraph-long sentences laden with colons and semicolons and an epidemic of commas. As a newspaper reporter, I had to unlearn all of it.

Years later, when my own children were infants, Dad and I spoke on the phone while I nursed, discussing *The Phenomenology*. We made it partway through the introduction, and then life intruded. Still, he attempted on several occasions to explain Hegel's dialectic to the girls. And the rules of pinochle. He would lean in close to them and speak with patience, like a favorite teacher. A Bloody Mary by his side, he'd deal the cards with his soft square hands, an insistent wave of dark hair dangling across his brow. He had a wholly non-threatening presence, a small man, a little doughy on the edges, with a deep tan in summer and kind, nut-brown eyes.

Seth possessed a similar allure, but I chose him because, unlike my father, he appeared to be so steady and secure.

Part of that illusion came from the fact that Seth believed he should deal with his issues alone, and he often did. "Just fix it," was a familiar refrain. Not only did he repair broken objects, he'd anticipate which systems might go haywire and fix those, too. He re-configured the toaster oven to turn off automatically after 30 minutes in case we forgot about it. He'd tell our kids: "I can fix anything except a broken heart." He seemed to believe this. So we believed him too. Sorting through his office after he died, I found a small wooden box labeled: "Things to fix." It cradled the girls' broken necklaces and ceramic figurines and bits of long-forgotten toys.

Chapter 6

The Math Packet

As that first summer stretched on, my afternoon phone calls to experts became more frantic. I wanted to establish systems that might enable the girls and I to survive in a world upended. And I believed that the right calls would make this happen. I arranged meetings with their teachers to brief them on Seth's death, talked to various therapists about warning signs of deteriorating mental health, and interviewed psychiatrists for myself. I signed us up for a grief group near home, a place where children and parents could talk to teach other about loss. Julia was game: always up for a directed art project to express her feelings or jumping it out on a mini-trampoline. Sophia, on the other hand, obediently endured the first grief exercise, something with pipe cleaners, and then made her feelings perfectly clear: "There's no way I'm going back."

Bereft and desperate myself, I thought maybe sex might offer an escape. I called the poet in LA I'd flirted with before marrying Seth. I hadn't seen him in years, but now I was unrestrained and in need of a soothing touch. This guy was, in many ways, my male twin: dark and brooding, a writer who could drum up the heat between us in an instant. We'd talk on the phone back then and he'd imagine me up against a wall, holding the back of my head with one hand and my ass with another. I could smell his sweat. We would have been disastrous together, but that never diminished our attraction; it probably increased it. "Just get on a plane," I told him. "Be spontaneous." Never mind his girlfriend—I didn't care, I had bigger problems, I believed, and deserved a break. Now, however, he faltered. Perhaps my desperation made him coldly rational. "Maybe it's not the best time," he said, squirmily.

Before I knew it, late August arrived, and mornings on the Cape turned cool. We wore sweaters and jeans on our trips to Mac's on the pier for lobster rolls and Portuguese kale soup. I started to plan for our trip home. The day before Labor Day, I packed up the car, a Subaru that Seth and I had bought just a few months earlier. I stuffed the backseat with snacks and games and pillows and plastic bags full of beach shells the girls had collected. I was scared to return home, still not ready to face reality as a single mother, but my fear was grounded by annoyance and resentment. As I lugged our not-fully-zipped suitcases out of the house, I let the door slam hard behind me: *I'll never have help with the bags again*, I thought. Instead of thanking my mother for taking us in for two months, I was curt when I bid her goodbye, still stuck in my own bubble of sorrow.

The girls in the back seat, I turned right, off Cranberry Hollow Road and onto Route 6. The reality of school, work and life without Seth lay ahead. I clenched my jaw tight.

When Seth died, we lost our in-house math guy. On the scale of our losses, this was perhaps a trivial thing. Yet even on that first afternoon, as news of his suicide reverberated through the family, and amongst his colleagues, while bouquets of white lilies and pans of macaroni and cheese arrived on our doorstep, I remember thinking: *Who will help the girls with math?*

Over the summer, Sophia had read 42 books. Her taste was eclectic: an old paperback on the life of Helen Keller; *The Stories Dark and Grim*; and a troubling young-adult novel called *Dorothy Must Die*. She acknowledged later that her reading binge had kept her brain busy, allowed her to push away terrible thoughts. But she'd also worked hard on her summer math packet: a stack of worksheets due at the start of sixth grade. My approach to rules and homework during that time was lax. But Sophia, a diligent student, took her math assignment seriously. Finishing it had become something of an obsession. In the car, Sophia leaned over the final problems, pencil in hand. She'd completed 12 of the 15 pages and was determined to wrap things up.

We slid into the line of slow, heavy traffic along with thousands of other vacationers making the exodus back to their workaday lives. I peeked into other cars, envious when I spied a couple with their children. Unlike me, they could trade off driving shifts, keep each other alert with chatter about plans and logistics for their bustling, happy, two-parent world.

About 30 minutes down the road, Sophia screamed. "A spider's on my math packet!" I caught a glimpse of her in the rearview mirror, shaking the pages vigorously with her left hand. She opened the window with her right, waved the packet around and tried to throw the spider off. I spied the white sheets of paper fluttering out the window. They floated over Route 6, descended into the traffic, only to alight again in the mild winds.

All summer, I'd struggled to keep my anxiety in check—or at least invisible to the children. Yet, with last minute packing and the anticipation of rebuilding a domestic life without our foundation, a terrible dread weighed on me. Now Sophia's wailing crescendoed: "My math packet! My math packet! We have to stop!" Her screams pricked my built-up tension, anger whooshed out like air from a party balloon. All the checks and balances parents rely on to keep from losing it disintegrated.

"We can't stop!" I screamed back. "We're in the middle of the fucking highway. Look at the traffic."

Sophia erupted into tears. "But I need it! I need my math packet!"

I lost control. I let loose the kind of hollering that is unacceptable, but once unleashed, is unstoppable. "I can't deal with this!" I yelled. "I can't! I can't get your math packet! You'll have to do the work again."

I began to cry at my own meanness, then Julia started crying. "Isn't Daddy's death enough? Why can't we all just get along?" she pleaded. I whimpered, they wailed, there in the traffic, on our way home without our math guy.

In Eastham, I pulled over onto a dirt road, and laid my head down on the steering wheel. I tried to breathe.

"Okay, we have to calm down." I looked back and saw my daughters' distorted, tear-stained faces. They seemed little again, their staccato gulps and whimpers reminders of a lost past: a fall off the swing, a scrape on a table's sharp corner.

Julia had joined forces with her sister in begging to retrace our path. "Could we? Please." After a silent moment, I finally spoke. "Girls, I'm going to do something I don't normally do. But I think Daddy would have done it." I took another breath. "I'm going to turn around and we'll search for the papers."

So I circled back and headed east on Route 6, past Arnold's mini-golf and the Elks Club. On the road, I mustered Seth's resolve, his determination to fix the problem, to be the hero. Many times, he'd gone searching on the beach for the lost earring or the delicate, handmade bracelet that had slipped off in the waves. He'd gather his snorkeling gear, and we'd watch him dip under the water. Sometimes he searched on and off for hours, and often, miraculously, he found the elusive trinket, the dangly single earring or special bead.

He'd call the girls over, looking crestfallen, and coyly say, "Couldn't find it." Then he'd spin around and shake his booty, laughing, the found object jiggling on his waistband. The girls would squeal at their great fortune: their dad, with his uncanny ability to turn bad situations into triumphs.

As we drove, I made a deal with the kids. "If we don't find these pages easily, you'll just have to let go. We'll get home and, Sophia, you will redo the work. And if the pages are on the highway, we can't get them. I am not going to pick up pieces of paper in oncoming traffic." They agreed.

We continued on for a mile or two. Then, on a small patch of sandy shoulder, I saw a line of white shapes. Sophia pointed, "What's that?" She rolled down the window and stuck half her body out. I pulled over, and even before I turned off the engine, she had unbuckled her seatbelt and flung open her door. There, along the side of the road, sheets of paper lined up like little ducks on a lake. Twelve in a row. The girls lunged and dove, gathering. I joined them, and we all three skipped in a circle together, each shaking a cluster of sheets in our hands, waving them in the air. Tire marks smeared them, their edges had been torn and crumpled. But we'd found them. We screamed; we jumped up and down. I twirled each girl around and we spun, heads up, feeling the late-summer sun on our skin, the traffic pulsing by. We sang: "The math packet, the math packet. We found the math packet!"

Looking back, I think this was one of the first moments after Seth's death in which I felt a little hope. Our math guy, he'd flown out of our grasp and then out of sight, inexplicably and suddenly, and we'd been left alone, helpless. But somehow, that day, the three of us bound together had stumbled across something we needed: those scruffy, tire-marked pages. Maybe, I thought, just maybe, we can pick up the bits of our lives—our pages, our work, our stories, things dear—smooth out the crumpled sheets, clear off the dirt, and begin to reassemble what we cherished.

Chapter 7

The Word "Suicide"

With the children set to start school, my big fear was that they would overhear the word "suicide" whispered among classmates or teachers and not know how to react. I was determined to establish a plan for when this happened. They'd heard the word in the early days after Seth's death, but I felt this moment required a far more direct approach.

It was a warm afternoon, humid and hazy. The kids were busy gathering school supplies in their new zip pouches, pink and black with various girl-power messages, when I summoned them to the living room, patting the apricot couch in a gesture to come sit with me. Julia jumped up and settled cross-legged, her knee touching mine, while Sophia positioned herself at a distance, wary, perhaps, of me ambushing her without proper warning. She remained standing, about as far as she could be from us while still touching the tip of the L-shaped sofa.

"I need for the two of you to understand a word that you might hear in school," I said, shifting my focus from one girl to the other, trying to speak to each of them equally. "The word is suicide. I know you've heard it, but do you know what it means?"

"It means killing yourself," said Julia promptly.

"That's right," I said. "Sophia, you know it too, right?" She was silent, simmering. Among the more obvious discomforts of this conversation, I'd also pulled her away from one of her favorite rituals: first-day-of-school prep. "Yeah, of course I do," she huffed.

My many consults with experts over the summer had yielded a consensus on messaging: Seth's suicide was the symptom of an illness that he could not overcome. He did not wake up one morning and decide to abandon his family.

"Okay, so you know that's how Daddy died, but it was because of the sickness in his brain. A lot of people don't really understand that, but I hope you do. And you do not have to talk about it with anyone. Or you can, if you want to. It's for you to decide."

"Okay, Mama," Julia said, rolling over her legs to inch herself even closer to me. I put my hand on her arm and gave her a gentle squeeze, trying to gauge the trauma I might already be inflicting with this discussion. I so wanted to stop the talk immediately, end it with some confidence that I could still comfort them. But I knew I'd have to say more.

"So, now, if you have any questions, or want to know more, like exactly how he died, you can ask," I continued. "You can ask me anything."

Sophia exploded. She kicked the couch and marched to the front door, yanking it open. "What," she yelled, "did he jump off a bridge?" And with that she stormed out of the house, slamming the door shut behind her.

I remained still, nonresponsive. I honestly didn't know if she knew the truth about how he'd died, or if she was just casting the most preposterous explanation out there, trying to show me how much pain my attempt at open dialogue was causing her.

I rose and walked toward the door, opened it and saw Sophia huddled on the bottom step.

"Honey, I'm sorry. Do you want to keep talking?"

"No," she said flatly. She stood up, refused to look at me, and pushed past, back into the house and up the stairs to her room. Behind the closed door, I imagined how hard her brain was working to not think about what I'd said.

When I'd finally taken the girls to Seth's grave, without the crush of relatives at the public burial, Sophia had dropped to her knees on the dirt and made a promise: "Daddy," she'd said. "Whatever happened, and whatever happens, I will always love you." I would later realize how steadfast she remained in her reverence for her father, taping pictures of him and a little note he'd written her, on her bedroom wall. For now, though, she would rein in her focus. It would soothe her to fixate instead on the new navy-blue sports shorts and oversized jersey she'd wear on the first day of sixth grade, laying them out on her bed as if on a life-sized doll. Her pencil case was full. She planned to wake up early the next morning to begin the new year.

I would leave Sophia to her thoughts for the night, but I assumed one day soon, I'd send both kids to therapy. Emoting with strangers in small offices is what people I knew did—people from New York with psychologically-inclined parents who primal screamed and practiced emotional armor-busting and lined their bookshelves with tomes on self-help and all manner of alternative mind-expanding experiences. People who actually considered that an orgasm might cure cancer.

As a depressed high school student, I trekked to a therapist on the Upper West Side, a protégé of Anna Freud who wore ballooning, earth-toned flannel smocks. I would tell her I felt fat, and then on the way to the subway back home, I'd stop by the bulk section of the A&P, fill a plastic bag full of sickly-sweet yogurt covered almonds and eat them on the street when no one was looking. This therapist suggested my family join us for sessions. In what I remember as a dreadful exercise in psychic torture, my mother and brother would attend my therapy appointment one week, followed by my father, stepmother and brother the next. In one memorable session that centered on complaints about my sullen behavior, my mother got so angry she marched out of the office. "And that," I said, shrugging my shoulders when the therapist asked if we thought Mom would return, "is why I'm so fucked up."

Therapy didn't fix me. What saved me in high school wasn't cerebral at all: It was, in fact, the physical expression of dancing—the visceral satisfaction of matching a movement to an audible beat, the focused momentum of arm twists and hip swivels and orchestrated falls to the floor. In particular, it was a dance teacher who saved me, saw something in me, as wonderful teachers do, and I flourished.

Throughout high school, and into college, we danced all over the city. At the Soldiers and Sailors monument in Riverside Park, half a dozen of us threw beach balls into the air while jumping and lifting one another in complex arrangements up and down the stone steps. My acute awareness of my body in space—and the way I could control its motions—felt like magic and freedom. I began making up dances myself, and those dances became statements: when my father and stepmother had a baby, I threw a doll around stage. In the school lunchroom, I choreographed a dance on the tabletops, flitting from one to the next, rolling on surfaces where, just hours earlier, we'd stuffed down tater tots and called it a meal. At a black box theatre in downtown Manhattan, I performed a piece about leaving home for college that featured my mother as a disembodied voice nagging at me from off stage about cleaning up before my departure.

Over the years, my dances became packed with more and more words, and I found my attention shifting, increasingly, to the page. There was so much more to say! But I never lost my attraction to expression through movement.

Seth understood this. And I think the dancer part of me was an aspect he loved best: while dancing I was easy, flowing, patient enough to wait for the beat to come. There's so much love emanating from a video he shot of me holding 18-month-old Sophia in my arms, swirling around our living room to that ubiquitous song that poses the question: "Why are there so many songs about rainbows?" It must have epitomized for him the joy of our mutual parenting, and my achievement as a mother: a beautiful baby secured on my hip, swaying gently, our hearts full and exposed. It wasn't until years later, when Seth discovered a local family opera in which children and adults performed together, that I returned to dancing on stage. I became the resident choreographer for the North Cambridge Family Opera, and though the caliber of movement was more Hokey Pokey than Twyla Tharp, I loved performing with my kids. It began just for fun, but I would soon realize how our singing and dancing offered them an outlet, a physical form of therapy.

Chapter 8

It's About Time

During those fervid years of courtship, when Seth and I lived in separate cities, each weekend together was a romantic whirl. Once, on a whim, we headed to Provincetown, a raucous little beach community in summer, but boarded up and silent when we arrived on a Friday night in the dead of winter. We'd found one of the few hotels still open, and immediately fell into bed. In no time, the outside chill was replaced by the warmth emanating from Seth's body wrapped around mine. He was like that, a heat generator, balancing my tendency toward cold. That night we slept like teenagers, heavy-limbed, motionless. But our delicious repose was punctured early the following day by a chatty couple in the hallway hotly debating omelets or French toast for breakfast. I began to stir out of our cocoon, propping myself up on his chest: "Morning."

The sun was strong and already streaming into the lobby when we finally rose for coffee and a walk. The clear, cool air infused the day with a brisk sobriety. Seth was in a playful mood as the two of us strolled arm in arm toward Commercial Street, the town's main hub, which, in a few months, would be teeming with gorgeous drag queens and sunburnt tourists and coiffed terriers meandering past the historic harbor. Now, an antique jewelry shop, Small Pleasures, caught my eye with its inky, gothic signage and glittering display cases.

"Let's look," I said, pulling gently at Seth. He was tender in response, extending his hand, calloused from so many years playing Ultimate, to hold mine. Seth wasn't ordinarily keen on shopping, but he seemed unusually enthralled by the examination of gems at the little store.

As he asked about the vintage and provenance of various baubles, I spotted a small, simple diamond ring nearly hidden by other, larger jewels. A few of the flashier diamonds really caught my eye, but I wanted to come off as nonchalant, non-materialistic. *Who needs big when small will do,* I thought, channeling my mother's general outlook that life offers little more than "crumbs of pleasure" to be scooped up whenever possible. "Look, here," I said. Seth moved toward me as I pointed to the tiny gold band—it looked almost like a child's. "Can we see that one," he asked the bow-tied proprietor. I slipped it on and we stood silently, admiring it together in one of those elongated moments in which a murky future suddenly sharpens to clarity.

Seth tipped his head to the left and moved toward the far side of the display with the shopkeeper. Bits of conversation floated over to me, notably the words "delivery" and "sizing." I turned away, trying not to interrupt the process that seemed, finally, to have begun. We'd been dating nearly three years. *I've been so very patient,* I thought. We left the store, generating our own heat despite the bitter cold. I was thrilled and also aroused by the notion that my fantasy guy was going to choose me, not just for a weekend away, but for a life together.

For the next three months, I waited. New Year's came and went, then Valentine's Day and my birthday. There were cards in Seth's boxy handwriting proclaiming love. But no proposal. No ring. Had I totally misread the cues? I was 38, and soon he would be too. We'd been seeing each other regularly, hopping on planes to be together several times a month. We both wanted kids—we talked about it on the phone late at night, me sprawled on my antique couch in Brooklyn, Seth sitting in his front yard in East Cambridge. *What's the hold up,* I thought, with some frustration. Where had that little diamond gone?

One afternoon when I was alone in his house on Hurley Street, an impulse rose that I couldn't suppress. I snuck into Seth's office and began rifling around his desk drawer. I felt justified in my stealthiness. After all, I'd waited for so long. Sorting through the loose staples and scattered scraps of paper scrawled with his shorthand ideas, my fingers felt something tucked in the back corner: a package from Small Pleasures. I opened it carefully, knowing I'd have to replace it without any telltale signs of intrusion. Inside, wrapped in newspaper, was an even smaller cardboard box with a Provincetown return address. There it was: evidence. I hadn't imagined it. But for some unstated reason, Seth kept the ring hidden in that drawer for months.

At the time, I didn't try to analyze why. Now it's clear he wrestled with profound ambivalence. He was scared to commit, he'd even told a psychiatric nurse practitioner at MIT about it during the first full year we'd dated. A handwritten note I read in his medical record after he died conveys his anxiety: "Discussion of problem of intimacy," it says. "As much as he wants this, does fear being 'trapped' in marriage and kids." Did he have an inkling of the mental anguish to come? Had ideas of suicide already begun to invade his thinking? I remember sitting with him on the beach one afternoon during that time before our engagement. I was pressing him about marriage.

"Are you thinking about it?" I asked.

He turned to me, and said coarsely: "I'm not sure you can handle it."

I thought this was just Seth questioning *my* mental hardiness for the ups and downs of marriage. After all, I'd been in therapy since high school, with bouts of depression and residual anxiety stemming from my parents' divorce. In retrospect, I wondered if Seth was somehow projecting his own foreboding of what would come. Though he never mentioned any concerns he might have had about developing a serious mental illness, I did know that at least two of his family members, a cousin and an aunt, suffered from bipolar disorder. In the 15 years we were together, Seth never once speculated that he might have had bipolar. His medical record showed a few periods of transitory depression and anxiety over 20 years.

I just assumed Seth had his reasons for delaying a marriage proposal. I put the little box away, and vowed to ramp up my patience.

That winter dragged on for Seth professionally. He desperately wanted tenure to prove to his family and community, to himself, and perhaps to me, his legitimacy. His case was, unfortunately, moving slowly through what seemed like a secretive and frustratingly opaque process. Tension showed in his pursed lips, clipped voice, and general prickliness. I alternated between offering reassurances and giving him space. By early spring, I'd stopped asking for regular status reports.

Finally, in April, the phone rang on a weekday when I happened to be visiting Cambridge. I could see the ease unfold in Seth's face as he turned toward me with a smile. "I got it," he said. A guaranteed job for life, worthiness bestowed by his peers, the public acknowledgement of his credibility. I now believe that this professional recognition—the durability of it—was what Seth had been waiting for to move forward in his relationship with me.

To celebrate, we headed out to the Cape once again. It was a gray afternoon, and I was on a deadline, writing a story for *The Wall Street Journal* about the high price of AIDS drugs. As soon as I'd filed the piece, Seth put his hands on my shoulders: "Honey, let's drive to the ocean." At Newcomb Hollow, the parking lot was practically empty—so unlike the summer, when it was packed with families schlepping plastic floaties and coolers full of juice boxes and lite beer down the hill. Seth grabbed the faded cotton sheet he kept in his trunk and chose a spot on the dunes where we could take in the riled-up surf. I scanned the beach where I'd spent so many afternoons as a child and as a teenager, slathering oil on my arms and legs with the summer kids, riding waves for hours, and afterwards, spreading our glistening bodies out on the hot sand.

The sensation of what was coming made my face flush, my breath catch. From beneath his jacket, Seth pulled out a split of champagne and the little box. "Let's get married," he said. My long brown curls whipped in the wind, and as he tucked a few locks back, I felt electricity in our gaze, like this union was preordained and therefore, impenetrable. "Yes," I said. As I held out the plastic flutes, he poured the lukewarm champagne and we imagined our kids rolling down the dunes just as we had. We reached our hands under each other's sweatshirts, feeling for skin and heat, and held on.

The tuna wraps we'd picked up on the way to the beach went uneaten—we were too giddy, with too many other details to digest. We rushed home to call our parents, and then Seth's grandmother, Nana, still living in her tidy apartment in the Bronx. "Well," she said. "It's about time."

Chapter 9

Controlling the Narrative

Back in the late 1980s, on the first day of my first newspaper job, I froze. As a newly hired reporter for *The Hollister Freelance*, a tiny, afternoon daily in San Benito County, California (a region best known for its Garlic Festival and the biker bar Marlon Brando frequented in *The Wild One)*, I hardly knew what I was doing.

My editor had assigned me a story about the annual "Ag Report." After he tossed a copy on my desk, I scanned the first pages and drew a blank. I'd grown up in an apartment in Brooklyn, attended an artsy college in Westchester, and later, graduate school in Manhattan. I was raised by intellectual Jews, children of shtetl dwellers who knew more about the mechanics of socialism than seedlings. I took one look at the "Ag Report" and realized I didn't speak that language. My editor patiently instructed me to call the agriculture commissioner for a comment on the various yields of lettuces, grapes, strawberries, walnuts—kale was not yet a thing—and write up the story. The "story" in this case would be a straight news bulletin with none of the stylish, meandering, semicolon-rich sentences I loved. The "Ag Report" called for stark simplicity: Who, What, Where, When and How Much. I can't say this piece was at all memorable, but I got the job done.

I'd been a dancer and poet in college and had not yet been formally trained as a journalist. So, in Hollister, I relied on my instincts to dig up the juiciest stories possible. We were measured by our "scoops"—nailing down a story first, before the competition—so I did what I believed I had to do. If that meant flirting with elected officials or swigging beer with city council members I'd write about the next day, so be it. I spent hours at kitchen tables with the town's historic preservation activists as they plotted their revenge against local development forces. I drove up into the mountains above San Juan Bautista with a cop who tried to teach me how to shoot a gun while we chatted about his failing marriage. Through it all, I was aware of what headline might arise out of each particular experience.

My aesthetic was tabloid: I went for the dirt, the outrage, the head-spinning lede. When I landed a front-page story about the police chief, Lonny Hurlbut, found guilty of evidence tampering after ordering drugs planted on a local woman to bump up her charges, I thought I had the coolest job in the world.

By the time I met Seth, years later, in my mid-30s, I'd worked my way up the newspaper chain, hopping from the alternative weekly in Portland to the underdog daily newspaper in Seattle to *The Wall Street Journal*. My career at its peak, I was still motivated by tales rife with conflict, wrongdoing, even shock value, but I'd learned the rules of reporting and took them to heart. I fell in love with the stories I wrote, lost sleep over them and doted on every word, revising and polishing until the very last second before deadline. My first Page One story about the secretive U.S. producer of what was then known as RU-486, the abortion pill, still gives me chills; in my mind it's linked to those early days with Seth and our career trajectories rising in tandem.

In the summer of 2001, I traveled to Murang'a, Kenya and the tiny village of Bondo, where Bill Gates, through his foundation, was trying to impose strict business standards on efforts to vaccinate children in impoverished countries. Patients with machete wounds and mothers carrying feverish babies were asked for detailed paperwork before being treated at a one-room clinic where bats clung to the ceiling. I quickly learned what questions to ask and how to get answers. It seemed at the time, I had storytelling clinched.

Then, after a three-year, long-distance courtship, my life with Seth seemed to speed up. Between April and September of 2002, I got engaged, pregnant, moved to Cambridge, and got married.

By the time Sophia was born, in March 2003, the adrenaline-fueled, conflict-driven world of daily news reporting began to lose its allure. I'd decided to return to work part-time. To smooth my transition, we'd arranged for my mother to help out. She would take the bus from Chinatown, in New York, to Boston on Mondays and settle in to her "room" at our house—a corner of Seth's office with a foam mattress tossed on the floor. From Tuesday through Thursday she'd watch the baby, waving me off in the morning wearing her high-top sneakers and juice-stained sweatshirt while I set off in black heels and petite suit jackets.

I'd return home in the evening and often see my mother hovering over Sophia, cooing, half in Yiddish, rubbing her hand in circles on the baby's belly. I'd listen to my daughter laugh and laugh. This connection between my mother and my children would deepen over years; her dedication to the girls allowed me to return to the work I loved. But after about nine months of our early child care arrangement, when I'd grown weary of her unsolicited parenting advice—"You're letting the baby cry for so long?" she'd yell from her room in the middle of the night during our failed sleep training—we hired a babysitter we weren't related to.

Still, I felt torn. I adored being a mother and wanted more time with my baby. And—somehow related—I'd realized that I was losing my appetite for "gotcha" stories. Increasingly, smaller, more intimate narratives—raw and personal, like mothering itself—drew me in. I wrote about stay-at-home moms who built niche businesses while nursing and potty training their toddlers. And about women who danced through labor as a way to ease their pain. I grew close to a mother I'd featured, whose son suffered brain damage at birth due to a hospital error. This woman somehow rose above her loss to fight the healthcare system, and finally, after years, succeeded in her campaign for new safety standards so other children wouldn't suffer. I began to care more about the characters in my stories, and their lives, and less about scoops. After Julia was born, it felt even more impossible for me to sustain my reporting and also be an attentive mother. I felt pulled in so many directions: nursing, nap logistics, fact-checking, phone calls, trying to keep two small children occupied while I interviewed executives.

When I won a journalism fellowship and my boss would not guarantee my job back at the end of the year, I quit *The Journal*. Soon after, I took a job at the local NPR station in Boston and, with another mom-journalist who I'd long admired, started a health blog.

The move wasn't easy. I was enamored with my identity as a high-powered newspaper reporter at a top paper. Telling people I was a part-time blogger in public radio felt, frankly, embarrassing. My friends could masterfully juggle two, even three kids and continue full-time work in the upper tiers of power, traveling the world, achieving international recognition. I compared myself to them and felt diminished.

Over time, though, my new gig grew more appealing. My writing partner and I had free rein to report on topics that intrigued us: childbirth, neuroscience, food politics, the high price of medicine, how poverty can hijack your brain. Our best stories were about our own lives: personal struggles with children and anxiety and aging. We put ourselves out there, drawing loyal followers into broad conversations about gender roles, America's health care failures, and all manner of sexual problems. Our readers learned, for instance, that for a time I suffered from pain during sex, but then found relief through pelvic floor physical therapy. Google it. There are details.

Seth supported every professional decision I made. He even grudgingly accepted the stories that revealed bits of our sex life.

But after his suicide, I no longer wanted my story out there. It was fine to spin my life into material when the narrative concluded on an upbeat note, when the iffy mammogram turned out fine or the pain during sex resolved, and it was all pleasure once again. It's different when your story ends in disaster. Seth's death was grisly and incomprehensible; it would never conform to the contours of a pithy blog post. If my life was a movie, I'd change the ending, go with something more upbeat. But I had little choice. My relationship with storytelling shifted again. I had been a gung-ho journalist detailing other people's suffering, probing and pushing for salacious details. But when it came to my own distress, I wanted the details hidden away.

Not only did I want to avoid my story, I wanted to erase it for everyone else, particularly my kids. When I learned that the *The Boston Globe* sought to write a profile of Seth, including the cause of his death, I leaned on a journalist friend to kill it. When a local blog posted something about a jumper off the Tobin Bridge, connecting the incident to Seth, I asked another friend to call the editor and guilt-trip him into pulling the story off the site. I made it all about my children, but in truth, I believed, irrationally, that if it remained unwritten, it would be less real. I wanted to live in a kinder, unrecorded world.

Once, sitting in my car outside the kids' school that first September, waiting to pick them up, I yelled at the MIT communications director, bullying him into promising there would be no reporters allowed into the second memorial for Seth, a larger event that the Institute was planning. He tried to calm me down in that way men do when dealing with high maintenance women, a little condescending, with his words slow and deliberate, the way you'd speak to a child. "Rachel, I completely understand," he said. "And we'll do our very best." I have to say he did. The commemoration later that month, held at the large auditorium on the ground floor of the Stata Center, just two flights below Seth's office, was packed with colleagues and collaborators, students and close family only. I felt I'd won a small victory: the record of Seth's death was mine to control. In the same feral, attack-ready stance I now took toward guarding my children, I felt an urgency to protect the record of Seth's suicide. I was its sole owner; it belonged to no one else.

An editor once told me that every journalist should have a story written about them at least once, just to feel the same level of scrutiny and exposure that our subjects experience. I pooh-poohed this suggestion. I felt justified printing every bit of dirt I dug up on the figures I covered. Once, while I was reporting on a mayoral candidate in Portland, Oregon, I discovered his brother had shot himself—a detail that was arguably irrelevant to the campaign. The candidate asked me to omit this part of the story. I refused; I'd uncovered a scoop, after all. Now, with Seth's suicide, I understood how it felt to be on the other side. I barked at anyone who threatened to expose my loss. I didn't want to be marked as the damaged widow who, unwittingly, chose the wrong man.

Chapter 10

No Imminent Risk

The men had taken charge of the family reunion. It was the last weekend in June, just days before Seth's death. This was the second part of his birthday wish: a gathering on the beach near his parents' house with cousins and aunts and uncles across three generations, nearly 30 in all. Much later, I wondered if this was a subconscious goodbye to the extended family, or a test of some sort, a dipping of toes to evaluate the vast ripple of destruction he might set into motion. In the moment, though, the all-consuming focus was on paper products. Seth and Daniel, his delightful cousin from Portland, Oregon were the chief organizers, together obsessing for weeks about which compostable utensils to order, which family members would be assigned what meal, and who would stay where. Looking at old emails after his death, I found a chain of 33 messages, including a spread sheet of cell phone numbers and a Q & A on logistics. All the arrangements lined up with his engineer's sense of order and rationality.

But when the weekend finally arrived, and even as Seth threw a disc with his cousins' children, manned the grill, and initiated long walks on the beach, his mood, I noticed, was erratic. Slightly snappy, then withdrawn, then so sleepy he'd crash and take a nap. He began expressing new worries about pressure at work, a surprise since he almost always kept his troubles quiet. He also made a curious comment about our children: "I wish they could just stay this age, not grow any older," he told Daniel. I interpreted it as a throwaway line back then, just a commentary about their present innocence and its imminent disappearance as adolescence approached. Of course, those words became weighted with meaning. In a very real sense, at least for him, the kids would never grow up.

It's true that for a year and a half, the robot competition had consumed Seth. He'd worked diligently on programming Atlas to follow basic commands: walk up steps, open a door, get in and out of a vehicle. The late nights with students in a windowless garage on campus took a toll. His sleep had become unpredictable. His tinnitus, the ringing in his ears, had grown worse even as he pored over the medical literature for sources of relief.

And now, the deadline to qualify for the contest's next round was approaching. Seth had learned that the rules were changing. This would mean that his winning strategy for Atlas was no longer viable.

Dominating the competition wouldn't change Seth's life dramatically. "You have tenure at MIT," I reminded him. "It doesn't matter if you win or not." He looked at me as if I was insane. Of course he had to win. Tenure was irrelevant. Failure was personal. Seth was the third son of a judge who had high expectations for his boys, a quality that each of them internalized in their own ways. Seth had spoken with his father and the rest of his family constantly about the competition; they were all deeply invested in Atlas' fate. To fail, in front of his family, his father, was unthinkable.

He was unrelenting in his need to succeed. Once, Seth told me a secret that underscored the lengths he'd go to never fail publicly. I was unable to verify it, but it rings true: after college at Wesleyan, he applied to graduate school in computer science at U.C. Berkeley and was rejected. Undaunted, he figured out who had reviewed his file, traveled to northern California, tracked down the reviewer and suggested that the committee had perhaps made an error. He asked for a new evaluation, which was granted. Ultimately, the decision was reversed and he was accepted into the program, receiving his master's degree from Berkeley in 1990, followed by his Ph.D. in 1992.

I had no way then to comprehend how much Seth feared failure. I'd joked about the robot Atlas, but it was deadly serious for him. I have come to understand that Seth felt trapped by his need for success, that his own internal pressure to perform one feat after another in an endless string of marvelous tricks did him in.

At the family reunion, Seth confided some disturbing details of his struggles to Jessica, a family doctor and Daniel's wife. He told her his anxiety had spiked and wondered if medication could help. Stooped over a laptop, I watched as the two of them reviewed which antidepressant might suit him best. She prescribed one, Lexapro, and he ran off to the local pharmacy to pick it up. Seth took one pill that day, and another the following morning. But then he stopped, telling me that the drugs were making him even more anxious.

At the time, though he seemed able to redirect his attention back to the lovely warm days with family, the meal planning and cacophony of children. Nobody expressed any alarm about his moodiness. On Saturday morning, after Seth rose and went for a sunrise walk on the rocks at the tip of Provincetown, he slipped back into bed. We made love. It wasn't the hottest sex imaginable, but fine for a married couple whose kids were about to wake up and demand waffles. I remember it only because it was the last time.

We returned to Cambridge Sunday evening. Driving home, I sensed Seth's low spirits. "We are our own family reunion," I said, trying to dial up the joy. The kids nodded; he was unresponsive. That night, I made Seth promise to go see his doctor the next morning to discuss his anxiety and agitation. He agreed. Early Monday, he set out by bike for a consult with his long-time primary care doctor. Afterwards, the doctor walked Seth down the hallway to the mental health offices. I didn't know it at the time, but he'd told the doctor he was "in trouble."

The physician's note makes it clear: "Over the last two weeks, he has had that 'depression feeling' come back. He has felt hopeless and even thought about suicide…He has not been able to sleep more than one or two hours a night for the past two weeks."

That morning, after I dropped the kids off for their first day of camp, I texted Seth: "Are you okay?"

"I'm waiting for an appointment with mental health," he wrote back. I asked if he wanted me to come over, bring him some water. He said yes, which I didn't expect.

We sat together in the waiting room. Eventually, a psychiatrist he'd never met led him into her office. They talked for about 40 minutes. She then invited me to join them. I listened as she suggested Seth try the medication Seroquel to help him sleep and to quiet the anxiety. I learned from the doctor that Seth had reported suicidal thoughts. But he clearly said—he wrote this on the intake form, too—that he would never, ever, take his own life. He loved the girls, he said, and he loved me. He was deeply engaged in his work. He circled "No" in response to a question about whether he would act on his suicidal thoughts.

I believed wholeheartedly in that "No." I had faith in his written response to that specific question. It was right there on the official form. It must be true. Now I see that answers to questions can be fluid, turn false. That an answer can become nothing more than meaningless shapes on a page.

I often wondered what might have happened if the psychiatrist had spoken more frankly to me; if she'd pulled me aside to convey the full extent of her impressions. "He has had some suicidal ideation with thoughts of jumping off a building but states that he has no intent or plan to take his life," she wrote in notes I later acquired. Evaluating Seth's overall risk, the psychiatrist deemed it "moderate," adding that "protective factors include family support, no psychosis, no past suicide attempts, no substance abuse, and desire to engage in treatment. Does not meet criteria for involuntary hospitalization as he is not assessed to be at imminent risk of taking his life."

After the appointment, Seth's mood seemed to lift. He was eager to pick up his new prescription. I would then drive him to get a massage—maybe it would be that simple, I thought. In the car, though, I grew annoyed. "You have to take your health seriously and deal with whatever this is," I said. "You have kids." I wanted Seth to pay attention to his symptoms, not default, as usual, to denying these dark feelings. But ordering Seth to examine his deepest thoughts never worked. He often bristled when anyone, let alone his wife, told him what to do. Often, I couldn't stop myself. There were times, I felt, when he behaved like my third child, requiring guidance, a gentle push. Whenever I felt his disposition dipping, I'd suggest a break from work, or a long walk. Until the end, though, he remained stubborn. The more Seth felt ordered around, the less likely he'd comply.

I wish, in hindsight, that I hadn't nagged him. I wish I'd pulled over, held him tenderly, with eternal patience and whispered, "It's going to be alright, I've got you." But that wasn't our marriage.

In the car, Seth responded sheepishly. "I know, I know, I'm going to take care of myself." It seemed like a promise backed by some resolve. He told me the massage relaxed him. Once we were back home, he announced: "I feel like doing some exercise." He disappeared to the basement and ran on the treadmill. So began a mellow afternoon. Seth worked up a little sweat while I finished some work. Together, we picked up our kids from camp. They were hungry, so we got burritos to go from Anna's Taqueria, returned home, and watched *Despicable Me*. Seth was going to take his new medication and get a good night's sleep. That was the plan.

My mind often returns to this day, June 30, 2014. I sift through the what-ifs. Instead of focusing on the calm evening—the movie, our girls held close, a solid roadmap for the future—instead of reassuring myself with the checked-box on the form that said he'd never kill himself;

instead of trusting that our lives would continue along a predictable path, what if I had latched onto the more troubling details? "Thoughts of suicide," his agitation, the uncharacteristic reaching out for help. What if the psychiatrist had, perhaps, deviated from the guidelines, and insisted that he be committed to a hospital that morning, despite his resistance?

What if I had held him through that final night?

Chapter 11

The Luckiest Girl
(12 Years Earlier)

I awoke just after sunrise on our wedding day and tiptoed silently outside, gently guiding the screen door shut as Seth slept. Heading west along Ocean View Drive, a winding, three-mile road that hugs the steep dunes in Wellfleet, I set out on an hour-long run that ended with a dive into the sea. The sun had a bright, late summer strength and the air was fresh with salt and pine. My pace picked up as a surge of triumph coursed through my body: I was 38 and pregnant, a reporter for a top newspaper marrying a brilliant scientist. I'd just moved to the Boston bureau of *The Journal*; Seth was a newly tenured professor. Blithely sheathed in my bridal fantasy, I felt like the ingénue star of a smash Broadway musical, "The Luckiest Girl in the World."

We were married on the beach, in the tidy bayside town of Brewster, proud of our carefully honed vows of passion for each other, unending love for our unborn daughter and a deep commitment to our work. *Clueless* is what I think, when I think of it now.

At the ceremony, on a crystal-clear Sunday, we quoted Rilke and the Berkeley poet Robert Hass' lusty poem about blackberries. My brother played Dylan's cover of "Let It Be Me" on acoustic guitar.

Seth's grandmother, Nana Marie, walked him down the aisle. My father and I held each other up as he tottered with neuropathic pain that destabilized his gait while I negotiated heels on the carpet remnant we'd rolled out onto the beach. Swimmers in the bay seemed to back-stroke in unison, as if performing a water ballet just for us. The sky shimmered a brilliant blue.

Anne, my wise, sassy editor, officiated the ceremony. When she gave us the go ahead to kiss, I was aware of an ever-so-slight pause, an extra beat. I pressed into Seth's body just a little longer than appropriate, hoping to telegraph the passion and fertility of our union. Afterwards, I kicked off my heels and we sauntered toward the festivities. The sand and weathered pine needles stuck between my toes as Seth grabbed my hand. We intertwined our fingers tightly as we walked along the tree-lined trail to Crosby Mansion, a grand 19th century manor, painted the color of lemon chiffon, built by a wealthy alcohol distiller so his young wife could throw lavish parties. "Thank you for marrying me," Seth said, pulling me into the safety of his sturdy body. I felt protected and adored. But I wondered, briefly, whether all this heart-racing adrenaline was perhaps not so good for the baby.

I'd relaxed my no-alcohol rule for the day, and sipping prosecco, I leaned over and whispered to various unsuspecting guests: "Guess what? I'm pregnant." The double whammy of good fortune made me almost dizzy each time I considered it: a baby and a wedding! In a picture of us taken that evening, I'm beaming in an ivory gown, my first-trimester breasts spilling out between thin spaghetti straps, while Seth holds my bare, tanned shoulder like he'll never let go.

Chapter 12

The Last Day

On July 1, Seth woke up before sunrise. I suggested he try to sleep more and left him in the bedroom while I began organizing the children for day camp. Around 8am, he slowly shuffled downstairs, a little groggy. I asked him if he wanted breakfast, and he said no. This was unusual. He generally ate his morning meal with gusto; a large bowl of cereals mixed together, Peanut Butter Puffins or Wheat Squares and Honey Os with milk and a big glass of juice. Kid food. That morning he didn't eat a thing. He did review a few math problems with Sophia, and worked on a puzzle with Julia.

"Is it okay if I bike with them to camp?" I asked. Then, as an afterthought: "Are you feeling morose?"

"I'll just stay here and read the paper until you come home," he said.

The kids walked over to him and he kissed them goodbye. I think we kissed too. I honestly don't remember, but I like to believe we did, at least a short peck on the cheek. Then, I watched him sink down on the couch and unfold *The New York Times*. That's my final image of my husband, one I'd seen hundreds of times before: Seth in his flannel pajama bottoms, bare-chested, sprawled out on the couch, head propped up on a little pillow, reading the morning paper.

A beautiful summer day. I biked with the kids about 10 minutes to camp. On the way home, I stopped at Starbucks for an Americano to go—a cup of coffee I'll regret for the rest of my life. I turned my bike into our driveway.

Seth's car was gone.

My reaction was a sharp inhale and a vague sense of dread. At that point, I didn't know what happened, but I was pretty sure he hadn't experienced a spontaneous burst of energy leading to a brisk jog along the river. I didn't think he'd run a short errand, either. I knew his departure wasn't about coffee—he didn't drink coffee. Nor did I imagine other, still benign, possibilities: a quick chat with a student on campus, or a stroll to the library to return overdue books. In my bones, I felt something had gone bad.

I jumped off my bike, dropping it to the ground, not even bothering with the kickstand. We'd agreed on an agenda for the day and his disappearance was not a part of it. I made calls. His cell phone. His office. Nothing. I texted him again and again: "Call me, please. Love." I phoned one of his brothers, then the other, his administrative assistant at work, the emergency room at the local hospital. As my heart rate ramped up, I told myself that I had been through earlier versions of this—when he'd been late from an Ultimate game and didn't call, or when his phone just went to voicemail late at night. He'd always come home before. My attempt at self-soothing was not working well. I'd broken into a sweat standing at my kitchen counter, holding both the land line and the cell phone, making multiple calls simultaneously.

Then I dialed the MIT psychiatrist. She hadn't yet arrived at the office, I was told. I said I needed to speak with someone urgently and was patched through to another doctor. I don't know her name. It was about 9:40am.

"My husband is missing," I said, explaining that he'd seen a psychiatrist less than 24 hours before and had expressed some dark thoughts. "Should I call the police?"

"Yes," the doctor said swiftly.

I called 911, gave Seth's name, the car model and plate number.

"Do you think he might be a danger to himself or others?" the dispatcher asked.

"Possibly himself," I said, that sinking feeling beginning to dominate all else the moment she spoke the question aloud.

I called Seth's cousin, the police officer, and asked for help tracking Seth's phone and car. Next came another blur of calls. Texting, emailing…the walls closing in, a clipped, frantic quality to each message. "Have you seen him? Did he call you?"

A Cambridge cop stopped by to ask more questions. "Do you have a picture of him?"

I raced around the house looking for a photograph. I handed the guy one of Seth directing Atlas. "That's him," I pointed to Seth, as if the officer might confuse my husband with a robot.

Meanwhile Jessica—Seth's cousin, the doctor from Portland whom he'd consulted at the Cape reunion—and her family were at Logan airport, about to board a plane back to Oregon. I called her. "Seth is missing," I said, panicky.

"I'm coming over," Jessica said. She left her husband and two children at the gate.

I finally reached the psychiatrist who'd seen Seth the day before.

"Could the worst have happened?" I asked.

"I don't think so," she said. "He's probably just off doing an errand or something."

"But usually he'd leave a note behind to let me know. Or he'd text me. He knows I worry."

By 10:00 or 10:30 I'd still heard nothing from Seth. I texted that one last message to him, "I love you come home," tapping the keys hard, magically thinking the force of my fingers on these particular letters might grab him. Might make the words come true.

PART II

Chapter 13

The Widowhood Effect

Grief begins in the body. I learned this bluntly in the months after Seth's death. Your gut, knotted. Lungs, bereft of air. A booming heartbeat; nerves firing off random jolts of pain. This type of extreme stress response explains what's known in medical literature as the "widowhood effect"—the increased risk of death a woman faces immediately after her spouse dies. When the death is violent, that risk rises.

By the time fall arrived, and the weather turned cold, I'd dared to imagine that my body might return to equilibrium, that grief had migrated to my brain, becoming more an intellectual, rather than a purely physical, problem. The kids were situated back at school, I'd returned to work and a veneer of normalcy prevailed. But tiny injustices set me off in disproportionate ways. When I learned that my younger daughter had not been invited to a friend's birthday party, for example, I picked up the phone and lectured the girl's mother about inclusivity and compassion.

As I became shriller, my heart began to race. Even as I hung up, having guilt-tripped the mother into an invitation for Julia, the pounding in my chest grew stronger.

At that very moment, my old friend Rachel knocked on the door.

"I think I might need to go to the ER," I said letting her in.

Rachel doesn't panic easily. She asked what I'd eaten that morning. The answer—nothing but coffee—propelled her to search my cupboard and hand me a dish of almonds, then prepare a cup of mint tea. "This isn't a food thing," I said. "I think I'm having a heart attack."

I phoned my doctor, who had become readily accessible to me since Seth's suicide. I explained to her that my heart had been thumping uncontrollably. I could almost hear it. She said if there's no pain, it's probably not a heart attack. Just the sound of her authoritative voice calmed me, slightly.

I'd been planning to take a midday yoga class, and I reasoned that breathing and stretching might help. Rachel agreed to come along and she drove us to the studio in my car. "Are you sure this is a good idea?" she kept asking. I tried to breathe and ignore my heartbeat. But as I unrolled my mat and stretched my backside to the ceiling into a downward facing dog, I realized this non-heart-attack episode hadn't yet ended. The intrusive ba-boom resumed, becoming even more noticeable in the sweaty, somber room full of yogis. *Can they hear this?* I wondered, looking around. When the pounding grew too distracting, I walked out of class, leaving my mat behind.

In the reception area, I doubled over. The startled desk assistant handed me a few packets of orange-flavored electrolyte powder and asked if there was something she could do. I told her I had to leave. I tried to focus on the crisp, autumn sun as I stumbled to my car, leaving Rachel behind in the yoga class. I drove off, determined to make it home. Almost immediately, my chest felt near exploding. I could no longer control the steering wheel. My fear escalated to the certainty of terror.

I pulled over at a strip mall in Somerville, and quickly opened the door for air. Parked in front of a Dollar Store, I placed my feet on the ground and flopped forward, head against my knees. "I cannot die, I cannot die," I repeated to myself. "I cannot leave the girls without a parent."

I tore off my coat and sweatshirt, thinking the cold might freeze my heart to stillness. I had never before experienced this feeling of internal combustion, like I might literally throw up my heart. I grabbed my phone and dialed 911. The situation felt both literal and fictional: so physically real, but at the same time, like I was a stock character—the middle-aged woman felled by cardiac arrest, broken-hearted without her husband. Even my voice—sharp, hysterical—sounded the part. I blurted out the situation: racing heart, can't drive, husband's suicide. The dispatcher said she'd send an ambulance. Then, in a moment that revealed both my privilege and the fact that I likely wasn't dying, I asked which hospital they'd take me to. "Somerville," she said. Even as I sat there imagining my own funeral, I knew there was no way I was going to Somerville Hospital. I knew the rankings, heard the stories. "I think I'll just sit here for a minute and call back if it gets worse," I said.

After declining the ambulance, I phoned the yoga studio and asked the assistant to pull Rachel out of class immediately. Then I called Seth's brother, David, who lived nearby. Everyone showed up at the same time, and together we called my doctor who agreed to meet me at the MIT medical clinic. Rachel drove right up to the ambulance bay, and, bypassing the line, I was quickly hooked up to an EKG machine, with electrodes taped across my chest. As I lay back on the exam table, it crossed my mind that this was the most relaxed I'd felt in months. David had gone to collect the children, and all I had to do was remain motionless and compliant as the pleasant nurses administered tests. My heart stopped racing, I grew sleepy. It felt like hours passed. My doctor reappeared.

"You had a panic attack," she said. "Textbook."

Not a heart attack. I wasn't dying. I would be okay, she told me, handing over a new prescription for anti-anxiety meds, and ordering me to carry the pills around at all times. Rachel drove me home, and we decided I shouldn't tell the children about this incident. I didn't want them to panic.

Chapter 14

A Party for Dad

Dinners on the couch became routine as we struggled to adjust. "Movie sups," we'd call them, the kids holding bowls of pasta in their laps, me with my salad, re-watching Lindsay Lohan's *Parent Trap*, or some other plucky heroine on my computer screen. They say the first year after a death is the worst. They're right. Each event evoked our loss: holidays and birthdays without Seth; school plays with me in the front row cheering twice as loud to make up for his absence; Julia, standing up at a lower school assembly reciting a poem: "If Little Red Riding Hood had a dad, maybe things wouldn't have turned out so bad."

After a particularly fitful night, I woke up to bright sunlight, a hint of summer on the way. I craved something as simple as that warmth, just feeling good again, and wondered: what if we could revive a trace of the joy we'd had just one year before? A seed of something took hold as I dragged myself out of bed and splashed cold water on my face. By the time I'd tiptoed downstairs and plugged in the griddle, I had an idea.

"How about throwing a birthday party for Dad?" I asked the kids. It was a Saturday morning. We were all still in pajamas. The girls sat at the dining room table eating animal-shaped waffles. Behind them, little rainbows flickered on the walls through a prism Seth strung up long ago. The children were quiet at first, focused on their plates pooled with syrup, likely considering just how awkward such a party could be.

"Really," said Julia, "with a cake and everything?"

"Yeah, with cake and music and, you know, a party," I said, trying, in part, to convince myself.

Sophia went silent.

"How do we have a party for someone who's not here?" Julia asked.

"Well, we think about him and talk about him," I said. "The party makes us remember all the things we love about him."

Julia and I mulled over the adjustments necessary in order to host a party for a dead person. Sophia, resistant to the potential sloppy drama of it all, finally spoke. "Can't it just be a regular party?"

"It can be whatever we want," I said. "Just friends and food on a Sunday."

Soon the three of us agreed: we had a plan. With the breakfast dishes cleared, we huddled. Sophia grabbed a pen and paper, and we decided to invite everyone from the original fiftieth birthday guest list. These were the families who'd helped us endure those first weeks and months, a group anchored by a core of women who'd rerouted their own lives to save mine. They drove my kids to taekwondo and gymnastics. They listened late at night to my endless venting. When I sent around a note explaining I needed help clearing out Seth's office, they showed up early on a weekend morning. Amy took espresso orders. Hilary arrived with muffins. Sarah and Tal and Natasha were there, too, and Pam and Jean, all ready to organize my sorrow away.

As the eight of us stuffed ourselves into his small office, I pulled out folders marked in Seth's familiar square handwriting. One was filled with the girls' art, another listed the Italian cities he planned to visit. Hidden in a back closet was a picture of a bridge Julia had sketched in second grade. I had ripped it from her wall the day after he died. I wanted no bridges displayed in the house. We stopped to look at each artifact. We hugged. We sat on the floor, propped up against the wall, reminiscing. It was slow going.

These were the friends and allies I wanted by my side as we attempted to celebrate Seth's memory instead of wallowing in his loss.

The girls and I began making lists and menus for our party. There would be scores of mini-quiches and a case of pink prosecco. A chef friend offered to prepare an elaborate Sri Lankan fish platter with rice and coconut green beans and carrots with tamarind dressing. John, of course, would bring his farro salad, and soon every surface would be lined with cutting boards of exotic cheeses, plates of macarons and chocolates. Each dish was like a long-lost friend. Come in, we'd say, let us admire you as you dull our sadness.

That afternoon, it began to rain. Soon it became torrential. "Biblical," people said, amazed by the sheets of water flooding the streets of East Cambridge. Families ran toward our house to escape the storm and the party became a refuge. Crammed into my living room, dripping, relieved to be indoors yet still fixated on the forecast, everyone hushed while I offered a toast: "To our friends, who saved my ass." The children covered their ears.

That first, posthumous party was carefully curated. I read parts of the poet Elizabeth Alexander's memoir about her own husband who died suddenly, and from Maya Angelou's "Still I Rise." Taking turns, our guests reflected on Seth, his essence still vibrant in the objects around us: the little blue desk lamp and mini-robot bookends that were holdovers from before we'd met. As my friends sat hip-to-hip on the apricot couch, I remembered its predecessor from Seth's bachelor days: an army green burlap loveseat so tattered that the Salvation Army rejected it as a donation.

The kids, gathered around the ash-and-cherry coffee table built by one of Seth's frisbee buddies in his honor, clapped out a song with the refrain "You're gonna miss me when I'm gone." A sixth-grade boy stood on the stairs to deliver a love song he'd written for Seth; another boy handed me an original poem. Then the children grabbed chocolate cupcakes and ran outside to slide around in the mud. At one point, Sophia, then 12, poked her head indoors, pink-cheeked and breathless. "Mom," she said, "Can we start a compost heap in the yard?"

"Sure," I called back.

She shot her small arms into the air and cried, "Yes!" The kids, in a whirl of dirt and shrieks, gathered food scraps, popped back outside and began digging.

After the guests had all left, the girls and I agreed: our party was a success. We washed the grime off our bodies and brushed out our long, wet hair for bed. When they were finally asleep, I walked around the house turning off lights and checking the locks. Suddenly, I felt utterly exposed in this house with its glass doors and only me to protect my children. "A woman alone," is the phrase that ensnared me as the buzz of prosecco turned into a dull headache. I felt the glow of the evening begin to slip away. That familiar unease, a taste of bitterness, returned. How did I become the only widow at the party?

Upstairs, a desk lamp still glowed in Seth's office. I stepped quietly inside. But before I turned out the light, I decided—perhaps to consolidate my growing misery—to pull out the cardboard box overflowing with condolence cards I'd kept in the closet. The pithy quotes against backdrops of waterfalls and wildflowers arrived by the dozens in the first weeks, eventually trickling down to a handful per month, then a few a year. What got to me, though, was how many cards included words that made me feel worse, not better: "I can only imagine how you're struggling" or "I cannot imagine how difficult this is." Or the one that really galled me in its misguided assumptions: "I can only imagine that Seth's death comes after much pain and suffering for both of you over the years."

Collectively, these messages worked to set me apart. I was the loss freak. My plight couldn't even be *imagined*. Stuffing the cards back in their embossed envelopes, my anger rose. *Imagine it!* I wanted to shout. *Taste the fear and trembling; watch death break into the safety of your home. Tell your kids to absorb the violence.* The cards deepened my self-pity, reinforced my resentment of words on a page that offered no relief.

At the time, I had no consciousness that Seth's death caused suffering to others, too. No recognition that putting grief into words is an impossible task, and that these cards, while clumsy with abstraction and euphemism, were, in fact, tender extensions of love.

One card has remained dear to me. I've pulled it out over the years when I've needed reinforcement. It's from a writer friend and begins much the same way the others do, but then takes a turn:

"I was going to say that I thought it would be hard even to meet all the girls' needs (when you have so many of your own) but in fact this is the part I can imagine best. You, Sophia and Julia have always formed such an extraordinary <u>team</u>. You move through space and interact with one another with a special kind of tender attunement…. you are a team now more than ever, and the girls are very lucky to have you there holding them close, showing them the way."

I thought about my team, organizing a party for the man we loved, who loved us, now gone, and the odds against us. *Imagine this*, I called out, to no one, to the world, kneeling amidst a sea of sympathy cards that looked like so many dead fish scattered, hapless, after a red tide.

I pushed the cards together into a pillow-like mound and curled up on the floor. This rush of feelings was exhausting, I realized, and I had work the next day. After a moment, I dragged myself up and into the bedroom Seth and I had shared. I pulled on one of his frayed sleeveless shirts and fell into the sheets for a few hours of restless sleep.

Chapter 15

Could I have Stopped It?

I couldn't shake the question: Why did he do it?

I assumed if I poked and prodded hard enough, I could figure out the answer. As a reporter, interrogating difficult problems always brought some kind of resolution—maybe not a solution—but at least a deeper, more constructive understanding. Stories brought light, closure, the satisfying sense of an ending.

I began reading research studies and contacting doctors and experts on suicide. If that first summer was spent figuring out what to tell the kids, this next stage of digging was an attempt to get inside Seth's brain, to begin to track his self-destructive thoughts. This had always worked in the past, burrowing into the facts and identifying the right person who might unlock the secret. It took years for me to realize that this pursuit was less about the objective facts, and more about me: easing my guilt over his death, trying to make certain I played no role. Because the question, "Why did he do it," implicitly contained a dark flip side: "Could I have stopped it?"

I was excited when Matthew Nock, a well-known suicide researcher at Harvard, agreed to meet with me at his office on Kirkland Street in Cambridge, a few blocks from where my kids attended preschool. I biked over to William James Hall one sunny afternoon, and took the elevator up to the 12th floor. I momentarily experienced familiar, pre-interview flutters—part apprehension, part hope, an almost childlike sense of what's possible, that this conversation could reveal everything.

A kind, open-faced guy, Nock listened patiently as I explained my situation. As a health reporter, I was curious about his latest suicide research, but I was also here because of my own personal proximity to the topic. He was generous with his time and listened keenly before informing me of the field's shortcomings. "Clinicians," he said, "are no better than a coin toss at identifying who is at risk for suicide." Despite all the experiments and studies he and his colleagues were leading, Nock said, suicide remains, for the most part, a scientific black box.

He told me the story of his college roommate. This dear friend had been living in Israel, planning a visit back to the U.S. "I had emails from him leading up to this," Nock said. Run-of-the-mill emails. With jokes. The anticipation of reconnecting. Then, before the trip, the friend killed himself. Nock described his own guilt: "This is tough, it's what I do for a living. This is one of my best friends, and all my friends and family are like, 'How the fuck did you miss this, isn't this what you do?' I saw nothing."

This bleak disclosure felt oddly gratifying. Even the Harvard prediction expert couldn't predict this. Just like me, he was left asking questions that had no answers. Nock, intentionally or not, made me feel better: I am alone, but not alone.

"How close are we to solving this?" I asked. He said that many people are trying to figure suicide out, but the work, as science goes, is incremental. Nock told me about a kind of low-tech *Clockwork Orange* approach, in which digital flash cards depicting spiders and snakes are shown next to pictures of nooses and pill bottles to instill negative associations of suicide in people's minds. I imagined clever brains, like Seth's, might not be lured in by this transparent associative exercise.

Abstractly, I found suicide fascinating because of its profound violation of our basic human instinct toward self-preservation. That's also why it remains so misunderstood. In Western cultures, suicide is mainly seen as the psychological expression of unendurable pain. In other cultures, for example, among the Inuit of Northern Canada, suicide is often contextualized as part of a social phenomenon, a response to larger, systemic injustices such as poverty, colonization, or forced assimilation. Here in the U.S., some of the most compelling findings have been developed through interviews with people who have tried to take their own lives but lived. Nock has conducted many such interviews, and through these conversations with survivors, he has reported certain patterns. For example, people who had recently attempted suicide were asked how much time elapsed between when they thought they'd *likely* try to kill themselves and then decided to *actually* do it. The answer, on average, was about two weeks. When asked how much time passed between when they were *certain* they'd do it to the act itself: five minutes.

Five minutes to end one life and upend the lives of so many others. Seth made a snap decision, one of millions over his 50 years. Most were inconsequential. One was irreversible.

Nock couldn't answer the "why" of suicide much better than the rest of us. Such a basic question still stumps the smartest investigators: What makes so many troubled people carry on while others can bear it no longer? What, finally, pushes people over the edge? Why did my husband die?

"People get into this psychological space where they are focusing on the present," Nock said. "They are not focusing on the past, they're not focusing on the future, and they are experiencing great pain. They think 'I can't take this pain and it's going to last forever' and they can't tolerate it anymore. This intolerable pain, he said, combined with an underlying vulnerability—whether it's alcohol or drugs, or lack of sleep—can prove deadly. "That cocktail of things can make people act in a way that…had they slept, for example; if they'd had a different time perspective, they would have moved out of that suicidal state."

A momentary pause, the right distraction at the right time. That might have done it. Such a shift could possibly have moved a person from his doomed, cornered state of mind toward a broader perspective, the reassuring idea that feelings are like weather, just passing by.

Sitting in Nock's office, I envisioned an alternative ending for Seth, one in which a sensor-laden watch or jacket or a brain implant or app could have predicted, and prevented, his suicide. Seth would have appreciated this technology. Indeed, he and his students might have been the ones to build it. When he died, he was working on wearable devices to assist people in their daily lives—a vest that could, for example, deliver social and spatial cues to a blind person wanting a heads-up when their crush approaches.

My fantasy suicide prevention device would be easily available online or at any drugstore, ready to collect and synthesize the kind of critical data that a spouse, close friend or mother should have at her fingertips. The quality of his sleep; the frequency of "pain relief" searches; the tone of his voice; his daily protein intake; the beat of his heart; the stress level of a work call; the pushup count that day; the thrill (or not) of sex that morning; his road rage intensity at rush hour; time spent in the woods or near water; binge-watching patterns; the state of his gut microbiome; the stuck-factor in his marriage; the fear-grip of a warming climate; his heightened yearning to get stoned; whether his daughter got the lead in the play; how much he spoke of love late at night. The regularity of his exhale. All the things I'd wished I could have micro-analyzed to predict his final act.

Using complex algorithms to calculate emotional states and behavior variations, the device would speak with a calm assuredness: "Hey, man, we predict you may be feeling a little low tomorrow. How about a long walk, your mother's leftover lasagna, an hour watching your kid climb a tree. You are safe, you are steady, you are beloved. We'll text later to check in. It gets better." Perhaps all of it more effective than my final words to him on a screen: "I love you come home."

In 2014, we couldn't do this. Nearly 10 years later, though, researchers like Nock have made progress. For instance, he and his students are tracking certain patients at risk of suicide using information from their smartphones and wearable sensors, and intervening when danger signals arise.

Still, we continue to toss the coin. Heads, suicidal thoughts that pass; tails, you're planning a funeral. In one story, a man keeps his promise, reading *The Times* on the couch; in the other, he's suddenly gone.

I left Nock's office without a specific answer to my question, "Why Seth?" But I did gain a somewhat clearer understanding of this kind of desperation. It's a sense of feeling trapped, the intolerability of the moment. Escaping from some seemingly unendurable situation is the prime factor people cite when explaining their suicide attempts, Nock had said. "It can be physical pain, it can be psychological pain and it's often in the context of perceiving that things aren't going to get better." He compared this predicament to being stuck "in a burning room and thinking there's no way out...besides jumping out the window."

* * *

Seth's burning room was probably his tinnitus.

In the two weeks before his death, tinnitus, the perception of ringing or an intrusive noise in the ears, haunted Seth. He'd had tinnitus for years before, but rarely mentioned it as anything more than a passing annoyance. Then, suddenly, it spiked, and he became fixated on it. Was that the "two weeks" Nock referred to: The timeline between thinking suicide was likely and the decision that it was inevitable?

When I looked it up, I discovered that tinnitus sufferers are all around—about 50 million in the U.S. For most of them, the peculiar "sounds" they hear are benign and easy to shrug off. For others, not so much. The types of noises can vary, and those afflicted describe a range of audio intrusions, from "roaring, buzzing or screaming," to a "whistling tea kettle" or a "hissing snake."

The Mayo Clinic doesn't even consider tinnitus a diagnosis at all, but rather a symptom of an underlying condition.

After turning 50, Seth felt his tinnitus grow markedly worse. I'd wander into his office and find him poring over printouts of research studies: One suggested that by matching the pitch of the sound in your brain with an external tone, one could, in effect, cancel out the sounds. He'd listen to calming music in bed trying to drown out the ringing. But he told me it was getting louder and increasingly invasive, interrupting his sleep. I could see the toll in other ways. He became more irritable. Our children's joyful shrieking could send him into a sudden rage. The whooshing sound of wind through unevenly opened car windows made him wince. "Close them," he'd holler from the front seat, and the kids would quickly pull their arms in from outside and roll up the windows as fast as they could.

I helped Seth schedule an appointment with a specialist, hoping an expert could resolve things. But Seth died the week before the appointment. I had to call the guy's office and explain why we couldn't make it. After hanging up, I quickly decided to call back. Maybe this doctor could offer me a clinical explanation of what went wrong.

I had one basic question for Dr. Steven Rauch, an authority on hearing disorders at the Massachusetts Eye and Ear Infirmary in Boston: "Can tinnitus cause suicide?"

Rauch had the reassuring voice of a man schooled in patience, the clear tone of someone adept at simplifying complexity. He took a breath, backed up, and tried to explain to me how these internal sounds emerge. People with tinnitus usually have some degree of hearing loss, he said, and that creates a phenomenon comparable to that of a "phantom limb in an amputee."

"The brain is expecting an incoming signal from the ears," Rauch said. "And if those incoming signals are weak or absent, the brain turns up the volume in the central auditory pathways and you begin to hear random electrical activity in the brain, like static on the radio."

Mostly, people just live with tinnitus. Many musicians have it, as well as pretty much every war veteran who endured combat. But for one to two percent of sufferers, the effects are profoundly debilitating, impossible to ignore. It's like windshield wipers on a rainy day, Rauch told me. "If you're driving and the wipers are on, you don't really watch them, you concentrate on the road. If you watched the wipers, you couldn't drive the car." Tinnitus is like that: if you focus on it, the sound can loom larger, become more distracting. When that happens, it's usually a sign of severe stress or a deteriorating mental state.

I didn't truly understand what this meant until a colleague pulled me aside after Seth died to tell me about his own tinnitus, which he described as the nonstop whirr of a washing machine inside his head. "Do you want to know how bad it was?" he said. I nodded. "I told my parents if they found me dead, tinnitus would be the reason why."

On the day before he died, Seth told his doctor that the ringing was disastrous for his sleep. He desperately wanted, in those final days, just to rest. But Seth was not a whiner. Instead, he just grew more irritable. I tried creating conditions that might help. "I'll take the kids, you go back to sleep," I'd tell him. In the past, this had worked, he was able to make up for some of those lost hours.

For several months, we'd been in a pattern of completely opposite sleep schedules, which, in gradual but inexorable ways, frayed the edges of our relationship. I'd go to bed early, soon after the children, and he'd stay up until 2am, then crawl into bed, often disturbing my light sleep. At 6 in the morning, I'd wake up to begin the day, while he tried to sleep. A couple of hours later, I'd hear the shower running; he'd rush downstairs with barely enough time to grab breakfast and bike over to work. We rarely discussed the implications of this slow-growing bitterness about our conflicting sleep needs. Instead, we spoke of surface considerations: *Please be quiet when you come to bed. Please tell the kids I'll see them after work.*

I didn't comprehend then how this unyielding, bone-tiredness could so undermine Seth's circuitry, his very way of thinking. I wrongly assumed exhaustion could never cloud his understanding of how much he was loved and admired and needed. I believed that support would naturally calm his distress. As if fatherhood or marriage could shrink a tumor. But he was already locked into the idea that he'd somehow broken a piece of himself: that ringing in his head became a death knell, an auditory expression of his own failure. It wasn't that he didn't care for us enough; he cared too much.

People who die by suicide often come to believe that the world will be better off without them. Several psychiatrists told me that by jumping off the bridge, Seth was actually protecting us in his way: we weren't forced to stumble upon his body in the basement, or the car. I am thankful for that, but I still don't understand how Seth could subvert reality to such an extreme. How had he become so focused on his own perceived shortcomings that he wanted to obliterate his entire body, and all the good he'd created?

Chapter 16

The Other Rachel

Seth and I met at Logan Airport in Boston. I was 35, living and working in Seattle as a reporter for *The Wall Street Journal*. It was Labor Day Weekend, and he'd been dispatched to pick me up by my close friend, also named Rachel, whom he'd been dating. I didn't know much about him at the time, but I did know one of Rachel's doctors had fixed them up and she called him "the hairy scientist."

As I stepped out of the terminal, I spotted Seth immediately, arms crossed, one hip leaning against his beat-up silver Nissan, shorts hanging low on his waist. He smiled and waved, the rainbow coating of his cheap John Lennon sunglasses reflecting the sun. He scooped up my oversized bags without asking. Chivalrous, I thought. Later, I would wonder if Seth's death was some sort of karmic payback.

The other Rachel, still busy at work, left Seth and me on our own. With the evening stretching out before us, we settled into a booth at a quiet bar in Jamaica Plain where we talked over Sapphire gin martinis. He explained quantum entanglements to me (a sexy physics concept related to orbiting particles) and I was impressed by the flair he brought to defining science. I told him about my latest story, profiling a lawyer who'd gained notoriety for prosecuting E. coli poisoning cases. We were, essentially, strangers, and so felt free to speak intimately, with little at stake. I'd just been dumped by a guy, I said. He mentioned a difficult colleague at work. We were both looking forward to spending the long weekend on the Cape. He was heading to his parents' A-frame on the bay the next day; Rachel and I had rented a small cottage a few miles away. After dinner and a few more drinks, we said goodnight and made plans for the three of us to meet up at the beach.

From the outset, I was fascinated by Seth's concrete brilliance. He was an engineer to his core, a man constantly trying to fix broken objects. He was also childlike. I'd soon learn that he stashed an oversized bottle of bubble mix in the back of his car so at any moment he could let loose a mass of bubbles and wow a crowd of kids. Years later, I'd observe this instinct to play in action: Seth demonstrating to a small child the optimal wrist action for throwing a frisbee or taking on the role of lead prankster with his cache of knock-knock jokes. He was a cool geek version of the Pied Piper, a kid-magnet. He yearned to teach them—about the stars and gravity and how numbers could open up worlds.

But when we first met, I was mostly fixated on my own romantic troubles. I'd been seeing a man in Portland who wasn't that into me while pining for another man who was very into me, but married. I'd hoped my long weekend with Rachel would offer a break from these dating woes.

My friendship with Rachel had lasted longer than most marriages. And like any marriage, we've had tumult, love and rage. We'd met when we were 15, at the beach on Cape Cod. It was at that very same beach, Newcomb Hollow, where Seth would propose to me years later. Back in 1979, I was hanging out with the summer kids, wearing a chocolate brown bikini, which—as Rachel tells our origin story— made me appear much older. She was wearing some kind of Danskin one-piece, possibly forest green. Rachel and I were both reading the same paperback that day, *Sheila Levine is Dead and Living in New York*. The entire novel is one long suicide note. But funny.

The year after I met her on the beach, Rachel showed up to visit the private school in Brooklyn I'd attended since first grade. In those years,

St. Ann's wasn't celebrated for its radical, artsy curriculum and famous graduates. The students then were mostly neighborhood kids, and the school was still affiliated with the Episcopal Church. Canon Harcourt, the local parish *macher*, showed up in our lower school classroom once a week to tell Bible stories; the Jewish kids were sent to the library.

Rachel appeared in my life during a time of peak high school angst. Much of my fury then was directed toward my mother, even though it was my father who'd left. As a philosopher and intellectual, he was the parent most curious about my writing and schoolwork. In fact, it was Dad's part-time teaching at St. Ann's that allowed us to attend on scholarship. My mother, being a mother, was preoccupied with what I felt to be "lower," more base and bodily concerns—food, warmth, getting to places on time. This divide at home, our shuttling back and forth between apartments, left me wary, never quite trusting the motives of others.

But I was intrigued when I was pulled out of math class one afternoon to give the other Rachel a school tour. At first, I didn't know who she was, but then remembered her from the beach. Just as she recalls her first glimpse of me in that bathing suit, she's also able to recite exactly what I was wearing on that day at school, an outfit that struck her as massively cool and bohemian: an antique pink slip from the iconic West Village shop Reminiscence with a black turtleneck on top, white jazz shoes and an oversized bun perched high on my head with a pencil stuck through the middle.

Rachel had an alluring, boundary-breaking energy. We clicked instantly. After the school visit, I showed her around my neighborhood. Hoping to impress her, I acquired some cocaine from a local dealer I hung out with, a high school dropout with dirty-blond hair that covered his eyes and a perpetually raspy voice that suggested chronic respiratory problems.

The first thing you'd notice about my friend was her orange hair. Now, in middle age, her hair has mellowed to a kind of soft, light butterscotch, almost blonde in summer, but back then, it was a vibrant ginger, so eye-catching it became a central aspect of her persona. Like her hair, Rachel has always been wild, audacious, just a little too bright, like a strobe light in a synagogue. She's a force of nature who wants to know everything about everything: *Did you have an orgasm during sex?*, she'll ask, in the same way most people inquire about the traffic and weather. *How much did you pay for those earrings*, and, *can I wear them*, and later, *can I keep them? Were those fresh herbs in the fish, or dried? Why is that friend of yours so emaciated, doesn't she eat?*

Though we've been drawn in different directions throughout our 40-year friendship, we have, in important ways, lived parallel lives: raised by complicated, divorced parents and step-parents, we both became journalists. We speak the language of upper-middle-class Jewish girls raised by intellectuals, who came of age in the late '70s and early '80s. We smoked a lot of pot; listened to Lou Reed, Elvis Costello, the Talking Heads, Joni; and tried, unsuccessfully, to feather our hair.

Our antics and adventures spanned decades. We've been ordered by cops to put our clothes on while skinny dipping; driven from San Francisco to Brooklyn sipping Kahlua along the way; struggled to stay upright in the crush of a Rolling Stones concert. The other Rachel is a thrilling companion, but also, at times, a pain. When she wants something—and she generally does—she asks for it again and again until she gets it. Though infuriating, her relentlessness makes her a great reporter.

We can recount so many charged interminglings and story-worthy hijinks that a television producer friend once envisioned a sitcom about us: "My Two Rachels." It never panned out.

Rachel is the kind of trusting person who sends the man she's dating to collect her friend at the airport. My first vision of Seth had an electric, purposeful quality, like he'd been waiting there—just for me—for years. The following day, he drove down to the Cape to visit his parents while Rachel and I headed to the Wellfleet rental we called the "Love Shack"—a poorly lit cottage with squeaky screen doors and rusty pots and pans.

During that holiday weekend, Rachel and I hung out with Seth intermittently. He invited us to lunch with his parents, proud to share his mother's eggplant parmigiana; we guided him along secret paths we'd discovered to uninhabited beaches. All the while, a clearly detectable magnetism between us grew. When Rachel left the Cape to go back to Boston, Seth and I stayed.

At Dyer Pond, we swam and talked about his research and my stories. We sat together as the sun set over Duck Harbor, allowing our bare arms to touch. I extended my vacation a couple more days and he did too. During this time, I allowed him to convince me that his thing with Rachel was more over than it really was. I didn't question his side of the story. When we finally parted, we kissed goodbye. He asked if he could write to me.

Our sudden connection blinded me to the ethical boundaries I was violating. My attraction was that complete. I was consumed by need, speeding down the backroads to meet up, drawn to his magnificent brain and family-man zeal which became obvious as he spoke devotedly about his young niece and nephew.

When I told Rachel I liked Seth—a lot—she demanded that I cut off all contact. She was deeply loyal and would never consider stealing a friend's boyfriend. She was stunned and wounded by my behavior.

But I wanted what I wanted. I did not comply with Rachel's demands. I didn't even consider negotiating with her; it would have been too risky. I returned to Seattle and Seth and I started a long-distance correspondence. A few months later, we met at a boutique hotel in downtown Manhattan when I was in the city for work. He'd just undergone knee surgery and struggled with a massive leg brace getting in and around the small room. But at that time, we were breathless and steeped in mutual longing. No oversized medical hardware could stop us.

The truth is, Rachel and I had been so faithfully intertwined for so many years, I never imagined I could lose her. I was wrong. When I refused Rachel's wishes, and continued seeing Seth, she stopped speaking to me, wouldn't respond to countless letters I wrote trying to explain. I now understand that for her, there was nothing to say. I had ruptured our friendship. When Seth and I got married, three years later, Rachel did not attend our wedding. She would not see me when I moved from Seattle to New York and then to Cambridge, 20 minutes from her home.

Years later, I realized that these two relationships—with my husband and my closest friend—were, like a personal twist on the Heisenberg uncertainty principle, impossible to hold at the same time. On one level it was a cliché: I dumped my girlfriend for a guy. I made excuses for myself at the time: I was 35 with a ticking biological clock, and Seth offered a pathway toward family: a mate, children, a home. Rachel represented the family of my youth. I chose him, and an idealized future. At the time, it felt like the only viable choice.

I always hoped Rachel would return and continued to write to her. But as I settled into my life with Seth, other women began to populate my social sphere. These friendships were forged during my first pregnancy, when it seemed so very important to pick the right doula and find the best preschools. Later, friendships evolved around our kids' schoolmates, where a great evening was measured by how well the children connected. When Seth died, these were the women who flocked around to help me.

They closed ranks with love and reliability: they are still with me. But they do not share four decades of history. They were not featured in a dance I choreographed in high school, about the birth of my half-brother. They did not rush to the animal hospital when the cat at our sublet jumped out the window; they did not know the shameful details of my binge eating or fear of flying or that my nicknames included Egda and Roach. Rachel knows.

So, was it karma? It's not how I usually think, though it makes for a tidier story. More often, I imagine that foundational sci-fi tale about a stone kicked off a path that sets off a re-writing of history. Without Rachel, I never would have met Seth, nor had our children. My life would not have followed this particular trajectory: loving a man who was powerfully driven to fix the world, who died because he believed he couldn't fix himself.

Slowly, over time, Rachel returned. After I'd sent out a note announcing Sophia's birth, she replied with a short congratulatory card and a fruit basket. Then we agreed to meet. At first it was rocky. Whenever she and Seth were together it was cordial but tense. He and I rarely discussed his relationship with her. I believe he felt guilty but was reluctant, as he often was, to share his true feelings. Certainly, I didn't press him, not wanting to bring my own culpability to the surface.

On the morning Seth disappeared, I'd been working on a story. I'd emailed my writing partner to say I'd been too distracted searching for him and had made no progress. A few hours later, I wrote back that Seth was dead. My colleague immediately called Rachel. By the time she arrived at my house, the phone tree had ignited, and at least a dozen other women already filled the living room. But Rachel sprung to action like family. She sat with me in an office at Mt. Auburn Cemetery, alongside my brother and a sister-in-law, Jil, negotiating burial costs. And it was Rachel who spoke with unwavering authority when I felt I'd missed the signs with Seth. "There are people you worry about," Rachel said. "Seth wasn't one of them. There was nothing you could have done."

Chapter 17

Anticipation and Disappointment

I thought digging would save me. For years I told myself that the only way to achieve any kind of peace about Seth's suicide was to just keep digging. I believed that answers would restore the sense of safety and balance we'd lost. I craved that unlocking of the story. I see now that the digging was a diversion, a place to funnel loss. It was busywork, not living.

I think back to that first year when I was fixated on meeting with Seth's doctors. I wanted an admission from at least one of them that they'd missed the signs too. There was the internist who'd seen him for two decades, the psychiatrist who met with him for the first time on the day before he died, the psychiatric nurse practitioner he'd met with sporadically over 20 years. I wanted to pressure an explanation out of them. Where had the system broken down?

"When can we set up a meeting?" I asked the medical administrator when I finally got him on the phone. He hedged, delayed, rescheduled. In the meantime, I'd spoken to Seth's brother Adam, who'd leaned on a lawyer friend to assess the viability of a medical malpractice lawsuit. If these doctors didn't apologize, or account for Seth's death in some way, I thought, legal action might help channel my rage and offer another mode of digging.

The medical administrator continued to push back. Why did I want to meet, what was my agenda?

Honestly, my agenda wasn't even clear to me at the time. I wanted humanity, shared misery, but I also wanted someone to blame. On one level, the facts of the case seemed clear: Seth had seen an MIT psychiatrist on Monday and killed himself on Tuesday. Didn't that alone suggest some kind of liability? But by the time the meeting was scheduled—one year after Seth's death—I'd abandoned the idea of a lawsuit. In the end, what would it bring us? We had our house, the life insurance money. I was employed. Why drag my kids, and myself, through a miserable blow-by-blow of our lives and Seth's death?

Still, the meeting had the tinge of an inquiry because I'd asked my brother, the lawyer, to fly to Boston for support. His analytical precision, I thought, would serve to counter my emotional response. We reviewed our strategy the night before. *This was not an interrogation*, he reminded me. *Be clear and professional*, he said, *not accusatory*. The goal, he stressed, was to find some answers so I could begin to "move forward." I didn't sleep that night, cycling through my script, rehearsing my demeanor. I should not pummel these professionals with my central question: *How did you all fuck this up so colossally?*

That morning, I grabbed a little notebook and pen—the doctors refused to allow me to bring a tape recorder. My brother and I drove to campus and entered the generic conference room. The doctors arrived and, in our business attire, we exchanged pleasantries about the early summer weather.

I could only bear the small talk for so long. I turned abruptly to the psychiatrist. "Why didn't you think this was more of an emergency?" I asked. "Why didn't you push to hospitalize him immediately?"

The room fell quiet. No one met my gaze, which was more like a glare. Of course, the doctors were defensive. I stressed that my brother was only here to give me support, not as an attorney. But once Paul got going, the line became difficult to delineate.

I think what Rachel is asking, he said, *is whether it's a doctors' responsibility in any way to consider hospitalization when a patient expresses this type of suicidal ideation?*

In a voice that was timid, and not at all authoritative, the psychiatrist explained that she was trying to establish a rapport with Seth since this was their first meeting. From the start, he'd stated clearly that he neither wanted nor needed to be hospitalized. He was obviously smart, she said, and in his charming, rational way, he explained away much of his troubled behavior.

"I didn't think he was an imminent risk of suicide," she said, parroting what she had written in her medical note. She'd clearly been coached for this session, which aggravated me.

"But he had suicidal thoughts," I pressed. "Thoughts of jumping off a building. And a family history of bipolar disorder. Why weren't you more aggressive?"

Her voice cracked while explaining how very sick a person must be in order for a doctor to force them into a hospital against their will. Seth just wanted a pill to make him feel better, to help him sleep. He had vowed repeatedly that he wasn't going to hurt himself. He was articulate, calm, credible. This was a known problem within academia, the administrator who organized the meeting chimed in. Professors were so clever and sophisticated, they were able to fool everyone—even themselves—that all would be fine with a little engineering fix, like a pill.

I turned to the internist, an older man sitting at the head of the table. "You knew him for 20 years," I said. "Didn't his behavior that day seem different? More extreme? Troubling?"

The physician was measured, and seemed to have a pat answer. He said Seth did express more anxiety than usual that morning. That's why he walked Seth over to the mental health department. As far as this doctor was concerned, he'd done his job. "I would like a better answer too," he said. He'd seen Seth one last time, after the psych appointment, at the ground floor pharmacy picking up his new medication. The internist said Seth's mood seemed to have improved: "He said he was feeling better."

Then the nurse practitioner chimed in, confirming the party line, that none of them saw this coming. She recalled running into Seth on campus years before as he carried one-year-old Sophia on his chest in a BabyBjörn. He loved being a father, she said. She periodically turned to comfort the psychiatrist, who appeared to be the most distraught person in the room.

Before our session ended, it became clear that these people also lacked answers, and they were too guarded to speculate along with me. I desperately wanted to be bound with them in a shared sense of loss; wanted to see their guilt laid out on that conference table, hear even a whisper of true remorse, a murmur about failing to protect a patient from harm. Instead, I felt like I was facing a wall of practiced distance: this happens, it's unfortunate, we did the best we could.

I closed my little notepad in frustration. I asked if there was some internal incident report they could share. I assumed this was required with any patient death. They claimed there was nothing like that, or, rather, nothing they could disclose. I knew I should stop but felt a need to pile on. I cited quotes from his medical record. *Didn't the family history of bipolar disorder raise red flags? Yes,* the psychiatrist said, but she reiterated his words. Seth insisted he loved his family and would not hurt himself. He claimed he would never do the thing he went out and did the very next morning.

Ninety minutes of questions and, to me, unsatisfying non-answers, had passed. There were no revelations, just the pity of strangers. There comes a moment in every interview when you know you're not going to get any more. In this staid room, I knew, that moment had come.

Everyone stood up to leave. I placed the notebook in my bag and gathered my jacket, unable to look anyone in the eye. If I'd entered the interview swinging, my chest puffed with rage, now I was hollow, depleted. I shuffled toward the door, my head bowed. The psychiatrist moved toward me, closer than I'd expected for a perfunctory goodbye. She lowered her voice. "Your children are lucky to have you," she said.

I stared at her, wondering why she felt, suddenly, this need to connect. "I know this is not really relevant," she continued. "But I want you to know, my father committed suicide when I was five."

I startled and looked her in the eye. It was the most honest and open moment of the entire meeting. Seth's death had shaken her, too. This unsolicited compassion helped me. It was a bond, a moment of humility, at least, amidst this failed fact-finding mission. I left the room feeling sorry for *her*, and later, invited her out for coffee to talk more.

Over the next few years, I would contact this psychiatrist occasionally. I sent her articles and essays I'd written that showed my kids were doing alright. I admit I was trying to lure her in, trying to get her in a room alone for a *real* interview. She told me she was intrigued by the idea of meeting, but just couldn't. She needed to focus her attention on her young child. We never met, but once or twice, I spotted her in the halls of the medical building, and we nodded to one another, like mothers do, with so much knowledge hidden behind a small gesture.

Even though I'd given up on Seth's doctors, I didn't stop searching.

Maybe his blood held a clue, I thought one afternoon. I phoned his brother Adam, yet again, for help. He quickly drafted a note on his official attorney letterhead to the Massachusetts Medical Examiner requesting a toxicology report. The initial response was that there was not enough "specimen" to conduct the screen. We pushed. They said they'd try. Over months of waiting, I imagined an answer: something in his body, a chemical gone awry. Maybe it was an accident after all. When, finally, the results came back, my fantasy of clarity was dashed once more: there were no opiates or cannabinoids, no fentanyl, meth, cocaine, no illegal drugs or kitchen cleansers in his system. There was only a trace of the antidepressant he'd taken two days earlier, and some Benadryl, the report said. I remember him taking the antihistamine on Sunday night, less than 48 hours before he died. We both hoped something as simple and over-the-counter as that might magically help him sleep.

This cycle of anticipation and disappointment became a recurring motif through those first years. At one point, wading through boxes of old papers and relics in the basement, I found a locked safe. Stumbling upon it gave me a bolt of hope, a thrilling anticipatory charge. When I figured out the combination (a victory in itself) I felt on the cusp of a reckoning. But when I opened the safe it was empty.

Over time, and through cold leads, I came to understand that my situation could not be reconciled like a well-crafted news story. There was no clear-cut answer, no disclosure of an affair or financial misstep. No revelations from a secret medical document. There remained only questions scattered amidst memories, a relentless looping back in time, futile but still urgent, like scouring an old stain on a favorite dress, hoping it might one day come clean.

Chapter 18

Food is Love

The first time I met Seth's whole family, I'd chosen my outfit carefully: a ruffled, below-the-knee charcoal skirt and a soft oatmeal sweater. This, I thought, would telegraph a kind of textured, but modest, warmth. No one had to tell me what a big deal it was for one of the Teller boys to bring a date home for Christmas. I knew I'd be entering a protected realm, and once inside, I was determined to rise to great-girlfriend-maybe-more status. As soon as we arrived at the house, a grey shingled Colonial tucked in the woods that served as Seth's childhood exploration grounds, he announced to his assembled relatives: "This is Rachel." You could almost hear a drumroll.

Seth always remained tethered to his family. Through college, graduate school and his entire academic career, no matter if he was living in Berkeley or Tel Aviv, he never missed a single Christmas at his mother's table. I'd detected this devotion early in our courtship, but didn't fully appreciate the all-encompassing loyalty until I joined the holiday festivities that first winter. Unlike my family, whose celebrations were ad-hoc, and dependent on the visitation schedule, Seth's clan was wholly committed to their longstanding rituals. Holidays marked passages, but also cemented family roles, enabling a kind of consistent, enduring faith.

As his mother stepped toward me, she placed a hand on my shoulder. I could see her green and red Christmas tree earrings dangling.

"There's prosecco and cider," she said. "I hope you're hungry."

We drank in front of the fire, discussing Y2K and predictions of snow. And then came the meal. Food is a primary act of love in Seth's family. At Christmas, that first one and every one after, his mother's side of the family prevailed. These Italian women were a culinary force. Nana and her two daughters constructed the menu for days: marinating, baking, prepping. It wasn't just the voluminous offerings, though, that made the meal, it was also the precision and pride emanating from every dish. On Christmas Eve, each of the seven fish courses was introduced like a prodigy, a pigtailed child playing Bach sonatas in preschool. To start, there was shrimp cocktail on ice, served with two separate dipping sauces, one extra spicy with a few shakes of Worcestershire sauce. The calamari from the local fish monger was lightly seared in a pan, served hot and crisp. Anchovies sometimes prompted a story from Seth's father, not about anchovies, but sardines, grilled, and eaten straight off the boat along the Tagus River in Lisbon. The main course, one of the few that lasted over the years, was linguine with fresh clams served in an oversized white ceramic bowl, with parmigiana so fresh you could almost see its shavings quivering against the silver-edged serving dish. The cod was always my favorite, simmered with plump tomatoes, black olives, and capers. Seth's mother noted this preference, and for years made sure to let me know in advance: "I've got the cod ready."

The meal would last for several hours, with pauses for prescribed activities. During the first break, adults (and later, our children) were instructed to open a single large gift, and then summoned back to the table. Next, we'd stop momentarily while the sisters prepared the desserts—chocolate ricotta cheesecake; a grain pie from the only bakery left on Arthur Avenue in the Bronx that still made them; and a dozen varieties of cookies, small gems dipped in almond paste, dark chocolate, powdered sugar. And Nana's struffoli. Deep fried dough balls stacked in a pyramid and coated in honey, candied fruit, and sprinkles. We conjured up the memory of her struffoli years later, when

Nana died just weeks after Sophia was born. As we drove to her funeral in the Bronx, I sat in the backseat with the baby, both of us strapped in tight, attempting to stop her crying by pulling my right breast to its capacity length, into the shape of a fat strand of linguine, just so we wouldn't have to pull over on the Bruckner Expressway.

Christmas Eve never ended before midnight in those early days, after the espresso and limoncello and last snatches of dates, figs, and chestnuts. When we finally said goodnight, the sisters would still be busy washing dishes while the men checked headlines on the television news.

That first year of my relationship with Seth, I was on my very best behavior, wanting so much to be part of a tradition-rich family, this family, where the women passed down recipes on index cards splattered with olive oil. So, I ate everything. Here, passing on a dish had significance, and often triggered a series of questions. Why? Why would you not indulge in this pleasure, this taste that we've enjoyed for generations?

* * *

After Seth and I married and had children, I grabbed control of the food management. So often, instead of saying yes to the pleasure of pure taste, I said no with a blind rigidity. Perhaps this, too, took a toll.

We'd invited the grandparents to Sophia's first birthday party. I practically melted buttoning my daughter into her first fancy dress, with its a pink taffeta bodice and black velvet skirt. Her tiny feet fit perfectly into the patent leather Mary Janes we'd picked up at the mall. Seth's mother had baked a chocolate layer cake for the occasion. As she struck a match to light the single candle that rose like an Independence Day sparkler, she appeared luminous, as if she'd been preparing all her life for this moment.

I pulled Seth aside. "I really don't think the baby needs cake," I whispered. Up until this point, Sophia's diet consisted of avocados, bananas, strained organic vegetables, and breast milk. She had never consumed anything with sugar. *Why*, I thought, *would she start now?*

"What?" Seth responded, staring at me like I'd grown antlers.

"She's never had sweets before, and I see no reason for her to start now just to make your mother happy."

"But she baked a cake, Rachel. C'mon, one bite won't hurt."

We sang "Happy Birthday" and Joan began slicing cake.

"You know what," I said. "Why don't you put aside a piece for Sophia. She'll have some later."

I saw his mother's face sink. I'd heard her tell stories about the first time she fed ice cream to Adam's son, her first grandchild, and how the baby's eyes lit up, never before having experienced the thrill of sugar. Still, I was a new mother with food issues. At the time, I truly believed not feeding cake to my one-year-old was the responsible decision.

The rest of us ate cake. Seth glared at me but said nothing. As if to make it up to his mother, he asked for seconds and thirds, scraping every last bit of frosting off the paper plate with his fork. Before we'd polished the whole thing off, Joan carefully sliced a small piece and wrapped it in plastic. She then pulled out a pen and paper from her bag and taped a note on the cake that said "S." "This is for Sophia," she said. "Please take a picture for me."

Chapter 19

The Illusion of Calm

I would re-evaluate our marriage constantly. Intellectually, I knew two things:

Our marriage wasn't perfect.

Our marriage didn't kill him.

And yet, every once in a while, I'd see a man on a bike shaped just like Seth, square-backed and pedaling furiously, and feel that air-pocket drop of dread. I'd start to wonder, again, whether I missed the signposts of illness, ignored certain bits of information, like his escalating irritability, that pointed to a deteriorating mental state. But what I came to see as potential warning signs were, at the time, so embedded in his behavior and persona, that I never imagined they posed any real threat. His moodiness, sleeplessness, fanciful ideas, and dug-in positions: these were part of the ebb and flow of him, and us, that, over 15 years, I came to know.

Before he died, I understood him, I thought; recognized his blind spots and shortfalls. I was also certain I could compensate when needed.

This happened on one of our spontaneous weekend trips to the Cape, before we'd married. It was raw, and the wind was already picking up when we arrived at a nautically themed hotel on Bradford Street in Provincetown. On this trip, unlike others, we didn't care much about the weather. The main activity of the weekend was wrapped in a plastic baggie hidden inside Seth's jacket pocket: hallucinogenic mushrooms acquired from a friend.

It was fun to think about tripping together on the drive: we almost got high just imagining it. With his right hand on my thigh, his left on the steering wheel, Seth sped along the familiar one-lane stretch of Route 6 all the way to the easternmost tip of Massachusetts.

Our drug-taking history aligned to some degree. We both smoked pot in high school, Seth in the open fields and rocky streams of rural Connecticut; me in apartment stairwells and phone booths around Brooklyn.

One key difference, though, was our sourcing. I had easy access to pot from my dad, whose questionable reasoning went like this: better that his daughter get weed from a responsible adult rather than having her buy it on the street. This arrangement suited me, boosting my social status at school. I'd tell friends to wait downstairs while I rode the elevator up to the 8th floor, slipped into my father and stepmother's bedroom, and grabbed a handful of pot and a packet of rolling paper from their stash in the sock drawer.

We'd smoke on the Promenade, with its sweeping view of lower Manhattan, or on the roof of my mother's apartment. Getting stoned was one thing, but tripping was always too much for me—I hated losing control of my body and thoughts to that degree. Seth, on the other hand, craved that kind of sensory-blasting party. It offered him the freedom to let loose his emotions, a much-needed release. When he was high, his expressions of love could be so tender.

As soon as we arrived at the inn in P'town, we raced up to our room, tossed our small bags onto the four-poster king-sized bed, and laughed at the various whaling artifacts and paintings of 19th century ships hanging on the walls. We eagerly ate the mushrooms and set out for a walk to the Province Lands, the windswept, sandy stretch along the coast.

It began to snow, lightly at first. Soon it turned icy and hard—snow that pings your skin on impact and delivers a slight burn. We continued toward our destination, the jetty at the far end of the beach. I noticed the sand drifts swirling as the dunes began to reshape themselves in the wind. That's when I realized the drugs were kicking in. My view of the landscape darkened alongside the worsening weather. I looked out at the water, a deep, opaque navy, and suddenly longed for the clear greens and aquas of summer. We were here at the wrong time. But as Seth's arms tightened around my shoulders, trying, instinctively, to keep me warm, I forced my thinking back to the promise of safety and protection he offered. Seth hid uncanny strength in his compact body. And I knew if we had to escape from the storm, he could be fast: not a distance runner, but able to burst into a blinding sprint. The comfort of his arms encircling me was short-lived, though, as the effects of the drugs started to peak and the ground felt less stable. The cold began to penetrate my bones. I desperately wanted to get inside. Seth conceded, setting a quicker pace as we walked briskly back toward our room. We'd started out holding hands, as we often did. But on the walk back, we let go. I sped ahead.

Inside the room, I tried to ignore the portrait of a stern, bearded sea captain staring over the ridiculously elevated bed. I climbed on top, piled pillows behind my back to get comfortable. *Enjoy the high for God's sake*, I told myself. But I was gripped with anxiety. What if something went wrong and we were both so out of it we couldn't manage? The happier Seth got, the more fearful I became. Who was going to be the adult here? Who would call 911? Or drive us to safety? I began willing myself toward sobriety, resisting the drug's grip, calculating how much more time would pass before it ended.

My free-floating fear was unspoken—a prescient monologue that would recur years later in our marriage. When it came to domestic concerns, I was the nag: Who's picking up the kids? Did they eat? How deep is the cut? It was a role I took on intuitively, the way motherhood changes you, the way my own mother's rapacious caretaking shaped me.

Seth, feet up on a chair and enjoying himself in the big room, was deep into his "What-Me-Worry?" mode. He embraced the high, unaware of my simmering disbelief: How could he be so content and carefree while I was crawling out of my skin? I jumped out of bed and began pacing, thinking activity might metabolize the drugs faster. I wondered when I'd be firmly planted on earth again, and when he'd be back too. It was a feeling I'd experience again in later years: two adults, together, but only one in control, taking charge.

When the trip subsided and the storm passed, I asked Seth what we would have done if, for instance, one of us got hurt and needed help. "But we're not hurt," he said. "We're fine. Relax." Just like that. No anxiety, no vigilance. For the years we were married, Seth projected the same illusion of calm, a deeply held belief that everything would be okay. I tried my best to have faith, to share this illusion. But even as we slept, finally, the drugs cleared from our systems, my doubts remained.

Chapter 20

Warning Signs

On the day of our second annual posthumous party for Seth, it rained again. As everyone crammed into my living room, I launched into my welcoming toast, now a central part of the ritual. To prepare, I'd sorted through Seth's books and pulled out three quintessential readings. The first was a history of bubble-making, including chapters on the world's largest bubble, various bubble-making machinery and the best bubble recipes. The second was his Ph.D. thesis, *Visibility Computations in Densely Occluded Polyhedral Environments*, notable because it was dedicated to, among others, his grandmother. The third was a book he loved reading to the kids when they were little: *The Museum of Everything*. A flimsy *Sesame Street* paperback, it featured Grover traipsing through his favorite exhibits: The Room of Fluffy Things, The Room of Things That Tickle You, The Room of Very Small Things, The Room of Things Underwater. Those rooms allowed for endless possibilities, a stirring concept that captured Seth's general approach to life.

I also wrote a love poem. It was sappy and rhymed, so everyone cried.

These gatherings would become reliably concrete markers of time passing; they stood in stark contrast to my own sadness, which showed up unevenly, intermittently, with no systematic progression. I'd hear a child in a playground call out, "Daddy, watch me," and my mood would instantly dip. Or, I'd suddenly need to lie down after filling out an emergency contact form, when, in response to the question about a second parent, I'd simply write N/A.

Our parties allowed me to control which version of Seth to conjure up: the brilliant engineer, the devoted, cuddle-up-and-read Dad, the trickster. We are permitted this fluidity with the dead, to draw a certain picture. Alone, though, without an audience, flashes of him would emerge and then recede more recklessly. I'd discover an old video clip—he's the Beast singing backup alongside Sophia's Beauty. Then that movie would splice into another in my head: a moment, perhaps, when Seth's familiar, run-of-the-mill stress became unyielding. My digging brain would kick in.

* * *

Seven months before his death, Seth had been hunkered down at the Homestead-Miami Speedway, a massive NASCAR stadium in Florida. The MIT team had one week to test their robot, Atlas, before the start of the next round of the DARPA Challenge, the major, career-defining international robotics competition that consumed Seth's focus and energy.

I was back home with the kids. Each day, as I prepared their lunches and dealt with various friend-group dramas, I'd receive dispatches from Florida. Atlas couldn't open the door properly. He took his first step but was shaky. The wind knocked him down.

I'd become accustomed to Seth traveling for out-of-town robotics work while I stayed in Cambridge balancing my reporting job and caring for the children. In many ways, this was easier—no arguing about food choices, no negotiating bedtimes. But for this event, it was clear to me that Seth wanted his family around, a sympathetic audience in his corner. It was right around the kids' Christmas break, so I was open to swapping the frigid Cambridge winter for Florida sunshine, while also making Seth happy. The kids and I flew to Miami. We spent one night at a beach hotel, drinking virgin Pina Coladas under a giant umbrella while rainbow-colored parrots encircled us, before heading to the Speedway the following morning.

By the time we arrived, the place was humming with activity: there were little dog-like robots, flying robots, talking robots, all maneuvered by earnest students living out their childhood dreams. As we approached the MIT tent, we spotted Seth. The kids ran towards him, jumping into his arms. We kissed and he told me he was grateful I'd brought the girls, but he was clearly stricken. The muscles around his mouth clenched unnaturally as he spoke of last-minute technical glitches. Additional changes to the competition rules undermined his winning strategy. Seth led the kids to the snack table and then resumed an argument he was having with his co-leader, Russ.

I surveyed the scene. Undergrads huddled around laptops running alternative algorithms while the argument between leaders grew more intense. I kept thinking: *It's a fucking robot, where's the perspective here?* Still, I knew not to interfere. My job was to be the doting wife, the merry cheerleader, to show the girls their dad's important, world-changing work.

In an interview with Al-Jazeera that day, surrounded by his students and our children, Seth's words flowed easily. He came across as he often did, the hippest, most laid-back engineer on earth, generously offering viewers a front row seat to the future. Dressed, as always, in shorts and a T-shirt, he talked about Atlas and his daring feats: "I'm still in shock and awe over the coolness of it," he gleefully told the reporters.

I realized, much later, that this was another reason we didn't see his suicide coming. In someone else, such grandiose schemes—claiming you could build a robot to fix the world's toughest problems—might have been considered delusional thinking, a potential warning sign. But as one doctor told me, "It's not grandiosity if you can execute." Many of Seth's fantasy plans, as outlandish as they may have sounded, indeed came true.

When the cameras stopped rolling, he returned to work. With his jaw locked and his words terse, he didn't appear to be taking full breaths. I honestly thought he might have a stroke, which is what I kept telling friends and family who called me for updates.

When the wind knocked Atlas down during the competition, Seth and his colleagues sank. My kids got pulled into the drama. "Can Atlas have a do-over?" Julia pleaded, wanting so much for her dad to attain his dream.

It soon became clear that the "do-over" question required a lengthy discussion among the judges. I leaped on this opening, suggesting we let Atlas rest for a while and take a swim break. All day, Seth had promised the girls a dip in the hotel pool, but that kept getting delayed.

In the dusty parking lot, just when it seemed he might have a free moment, Seth's phone rang. The judges granted Atlas the do-over the MIT team had requested—some questionable error in the official timer allowed the robot a second pass. There would be no family swim. Seth was ecstatic. I was enraged, and insisted that he explain to the kids why, after they'd been waiting in the hot sun for hours, he wouldn't be swimming with them. He responded with an impossible question.

"Kids," he said. "If Daddy got a chance for a do-over, so maybe Atlas could be better this time and score higher, would you want him to take that second chance, or just give up and leave now for a swim?"

A moment passed.

"Swim!" they said together.

Seth's silence conveyed to the girls that this was the wrong answer.

"But it's okay if you stay here with Atlas, Daddy," Sophia said. Julia nodded, glumly.

Looking like he was about to implode, Seth hugged the girls, pulled out his phone and called to ask the judge for a 40-minute delay. Speeding off in the rental car, we hurried through the doors of the Days Inn, quickly wriggling into bathing suits and back downstairs again. Seth tossed the squealing girls around the kidney-shaped pool for 15 minutes. Then he changed back into dry shorts and drove back to the Speedway, leaving me with the wet children. For them, he was a master, able to deliver on everything he promised. For me, Seth's mad dashing here and there left an unshakeable sense of resentment. It was beginning to feel familiar: I did the grunt work, he got the glory.

In the end, Atlas squeaked by and qualified for the finals. After the competition, I took over the agenda. I tried to get Seth to relax. We headed to another beach town where I hoped he could unwind, play with the kids and lose track of time.

The two of us did reconnect, and I felt some balance restored. We napped in the afternoons, rolled around in bed when the kids watched princess movies in the living room. We sent out an impromptu Christmas card with calm turquoise waters as our backdrop, Seth bare-chested and serene, his arm propped on my shoulder. He wouldn't live to see the robot in the final competition; it would have broken his heart that Atlas didn't win. "Maybe Atlas needed Daddy there," the girls said.

After the trip, Seth's stress roared back. In addition to the competition, he became the de facto leader of a neighborhood group set on dismantling an oversized, asbestos-laden former jail and courthouse near our home. The Soviet-style, concrete eyesore never should have been built—it far exceeded the zoning limits in our residential East Cambridge neighborhood.

Seth and a former colleague mounted the opposition, meeting several times a week with a ragtag group of neighbors intent on outmaneuvering the city. They passed out flyers and petitioned local officials. I wholeheartedly supported the cause; the toxic building should have been torn down and converted into public space the entire community could enjoy. Still, on late nights when Seth plotted with the neighborhood activists, I was angry that he wasn't home with us.

Over the months, as his group racked up losses against the entrenched city bureaucrats, Seth grew more visibly irritated that the neighbors had been wronged. One night, I caught a glimpse of what I later speculated might be a form of mania as he came to me with wild eyes, saying he'd found the solution that would change the developers' minds. "It's so brilliant, so simple," he repeated. But as I tried to coax him to write down this grand idea, state it clearly, he couldn't, or, rather, he tried, but what he wrote was nonsensical.

I encouraged him to clarify his thoughts: "Just try to tell me, exactly, what you're going to say to win them over?"

"It's so amazing," he responded, "so beautifully logical." He was ablaze, possibly stoned, and it scared me. In the morning, the genius idea, and the wildness in his eyes, were gone. He hardly remembered the episode. To me, though, it was alarming. I later wished I'd acted on my instincts, perhaps called a doctor to describe what were likely symptoms of an illness.

Instead, I pushed to go to couples' therapy. Our bond felt frayed. Work and child-rearing and the strain of over a decade of marriage had left us both a little ragged. We'd stopped looking into each other's eyes, I realized, we were drifting; taking care of the kids' needs and financial demands, but side-stepping our own. I wanted Seth back.

He agreed to couples counseling. We had done it a few times, in the early, sleep-deprived years when the kids were babies. We both felt overworked and underappreciated. At times, our treatment of each other could get shrill, even nasty.

Once, after a dinner party, he was silent on the drive home. In the house, he confronted me: "Do you know how many times you said the word 'like' over dinner?" It was embarrassing, he said, and reflected badly on both of us. I felt ashamed and attacked and began to be more careful about what I said around him. There were times I felt I was walking on eggshells when Seth was in one of his moods.

When that happened, his prankster sensibility disappeared. After a wildly successful birthday party scavenger hunt for Sophia, the kids and their parents gathered at a neighborhood pizza place for an early supper. It was Seth's kind of vibe: paper plates, slices on demand, a giggling cacophony of nine-year-olds. As usual, he was wearing shorts, even though it was March, still very much winter in New England. "This is his teaching attire too," I said, pointing to his bare legs. Everyone laughed. But something about my tone, the turn of attention toward him, triggered Seth's ire.

Perhaps he felt mocked and shamed, a child caught in an act of naughtiness. He reached over me for the car keys, grabbing them almost violently. "Where'd you park?" he asked.

I pointed down the street. "Are you okay?" He spun on his heels and marched off. Stunned, I turned to my guests, who were, at this point, mostly my mom friends. "What'd I say?"

Seth's shorts, and his casual style, were a frequent topic of conversation. I had no idea what I'd done differently this time that so angered him.

"Rachel," said my friend Amy, placing a hand on my shoulder. "We all have the same marriage."

At therapy, though, Seth was surprisingly open, speaking of childhood disappointments, his deep love for me and the girls and what a great mom I was. Our eyes locked. "I want this," he said. I did, too. We left the therapist's office holding hands. He told me he felt lighter, like we'd accomplished something. He wanted to continue. But when our second appointment rolled around, he cancelled it. "Too busy," he said. "Work."

We went on with our lives. As my friend said, our marriage was no better or worse than so many others. Still, when I think back, I remember moments that showed Seth's capacity to abandon us.

There were small, inconsequential departures. At the beach, more than once, he'd sheepishly prop himself up on the towel and ask if I'd take charge while he went off to get stoned. "Sure," I'd say, "go wild." He'd prepared for this, carrying a little pipe and a couple bowls of weed in a cloth tote bag down the dune along with the pails and shovels and more traditional beach paraphernalia. "I'll be right back," he would say to the kids, and walk along the water line alone, until he was out of sight. They hardly noticed his disappearance, so certain he'd return. And when he did, he'd fling the tote bag to me, and run over to them, plopping down to his knees in the sand.

Together he and the girls would drip wet sand through their fingers, meticulously creating swirly castles with shells for windows and seaweed flags and stories about brave princesses who escaped wicked families and found bliss in their own utopian kingdom. I wasn't crazy about the objective situation: my husband getting high to deepen his sensory enjoyment of our children at play. But it was hard to ignore my heart, full of tenderness, witnessing the deep devotion emanating from Seth, on all fours, a child just like them, conjuring stories together. "And what's the princess's name?" he would ask, or "Do they like pancakes?" When the tide came up and washed over the castle, the three of them would rise, their bodies coated with wet sand, and step backwards for a running start. Holding each other's hands, set for a countdown, they'd wait for a "biggie" and simultaneously dive under the monster wave, soon emerging for more. I'd watch my daughters and their father from my dry perch in the sun, relishing this picture of unhindered exuberance, but also on high alert, ready to jump in and save them should the rip tide strengthen before Seth noticed any danger.

There were also actual disappearances.

We'd planned and saved for a year to travel to Greece with several families from school. Gathering documents together, I realized Julia's passport had expired; we'd have to renew it quickly. I asked Seth to dig up her birth certificate. As we left for the post office, I double-checked: "Are you sure you've got the birth certificate?"

"Yes," he shot back, annoyed.

The passport line was long. After about 20 minutes of waiting, Seth muttered, "Shit." He'd left the birth certificate at home.

I turned to glare at him and raised my voice. "Really, you forgot it? But you said you had it! I reminded you, like, three times."

Others in line turned toward us and stared. We were a cliché: a couple locked in a private battle that was spilling into a public space. Seth's lips pursed, his fists tightened. I vaguely remember him telling me to lower my voice before he stormed out of the post office. I'd soon learn he'd taken the car, leaving Julia and me on our own.

Infuriated, I called his cell phone again and again, periodically stepping away from the passport line to phone him while ordering Julia to hold our spot. When our turn came, I explained to the clerk that my husband had left in a huff, but I could vouch for my daughter. Couldn't he just give me a break and issue the passport without her father present? I pushed her old passport under the glass, noting it had only just expired. "Can't you accept this one?" Of course, he couldn't.

I pulled Julia over to a bench and the two of us sat together in silence while I tried to figure out what to do.

"Why did Daddy go away?" Julia asked.

"We had a fight, honey, he'll be back."

But I wasn't so sure. After about 30 minutes of unanswered calls and texts to Seth, I pivoted. Sophia was at a birthday party and had to be picked up. I called Seth's brother, David, who first collected Julia and me at the post office, and then Sophia at the party. Hours later, there was still no sign of Seth. I realized there was a possibility he wouldn't come back—he was that angry.

I began to panic.

Suddenly, I just wanted him home, to tell him I was sorry. He remained unreachable, and I began to catastrophize. How would the girls and I go on without him? My mind drifted. I could move back to Brooklyn, live with my mother. But that was the nightmare: becoming the single, angry, depressed mom. At that moment I decided I would do anything to get him back.

Seth returned later that night, with big hugs for the girls and no apology. Still, I said I was sorry for raising my voice, and took full responsibility for the post office fiasco. We needed him, and so I was willing to absorb all the blame. The following weekend, we renewed Julia's passport without another mention of the fight.

When we set out to Greece in early summer, Seth couldn't join us—his work on Atlas had become all-consuming. The girls were disappointed, but also distracted by a sense of adventure. We traveled with friends, and upon arriving in Crete we all jumped into the bluest of blue water. Our regrets washed away.

Then it got even better.

Atop the mountains at the site of the Oracle of Delphi we surveyed the rocky crags imagining Greeks and Romans trekking slowly upwards, posing their most pressing questions to the priestess Apollo. It was an otherworldly place, steeped in ancient stories, the deliverance of divine knowledge. Amidst this beauty, I had my own little secret. Seth had texted two days earlier: work was progressing, he found a cheap, last-minute flight, and would meet us in Delphi. "Promise not to tell the girls," he said. "I want to surprise them."

As we made our way down the mountain, Seth was directing a lost cabbie to the site. When we arrived at the base, the kids began jumping around the boulders with friends, begging for ice cream in the heat. That's when I spotted him, striding up the hill with his familiar, purposeful gait, shorts hanging on his hips and a yellow Berkeley T-shirt. I skipped down the path to greet him—I couldn't wait—and together we walked toward the children. When he saw them, he let go of my shoulder and began jogging ahead, saying "Woo-hoo-hoo" the way he did. They looked up, froze momentarily, and then, suddenly unbothered by the intense sun, raced to him. He picked one girl up on either arm and twirled them both around, reveling in his heroic achievement and their boundless joy.

"You're here?" they screamed. "How did you get here?"

The other parents traveling with us looked on, awed by Seth's chutzpah. Another dad had also arrived partway through the trip, but no one really noticed him. Seth, on the other hand, received a coronation.

As the girls grabbed his hands and began leading him up the mountain, I heard them breathlessly explaining the story of the Oracle.

"That," my friend Pam said, "is one amazing guy."

Chapter 21

The Video

The kids appeared to be managing better than me in those first years. They rarely flung themselves on furniture, weeping, like I did. Or imagined they'd been somehow doomed by fate to a future of loneliness. I'd tried to protect them from the more gruesome and incomprehensible facts of their father's death. They were little girls, I reasoned, and there would be plenty of time for the full story to be told. I wasn't lying to them, I rationalized, I was just elongating the moments before telling them everything.

I'd tried to answer all their questions about Seth's death honestly, but there were certain details I'd withheld. I didn't mention, for example, that his body clipped a construction crane on the way down, forcing a sharp sideways lurch to the trajectory of his fall. Nor had I mentioned the bystander who tweeted that he saw someone jump from the bridge. I didn't tell them about the plastic baggie of pot I found in his desk drawer that I hastily flushed down the toilet as our family gathered at the house the day he died. I never explained the explosion I'd had with my brother's wife, the girls' sweet aunt, one night that first summer we were in Wellfleet.

The blow-up was over a video. Amidst the whispers and questions swirling around in those early days, I'd overheard someone mention a video. Impossible, was my first thought. *How much worse can this get?* As a reporter, it was a salacious detail to pursue. As a mother, it was unbearable.

I don't remember who said it, or when. But the words were clear: "There's video of him falling from the bridge." Would this be the image that tipped me into madness? The source of future nightmares? Who even captured this? A random guy on the banks of the river, pressing record as he watched a figure fall, ready to post alongside his hamster videos on YouTube?

I called Seth's brother, Adam, the Harvard-trained lawyer and all-around mensch.

"Is there really video?"

He took a breath.

"Yes," he said. "But it's not what you imagine."

The footage is grainy, Adam said, from a camera mounted on the bridge that runs day and night. You can't see Seth's face, or limbs, just a small, dark speck falling.

The fact of the video made me feel like I'd been beaten senseless. Pummeled. I believed that when the video went public—and it was only a matter of time—it would haunt my children immeasurably. The final image they'd have of their father would obliterate any nuanced explanation I'd offered about his "broken brain" as the culprit. It might even obscure the truth of his deep, enduring love for them. There would only be an indelible picture: his body, tumbling down.

I had tried to bury my knowledge of the video, focus my attention elsewhere until I'd figured out how to manage it. We were in our little cocoon on the Cape, and I wanted the kids to remain there as long as possible.

My brother and sister-in-law had driven up from Washington to see us. She's always been the most gracious and understated person in our family. Unlike the rest of us, she doesn't interrupt, or raise her voice, or dump inappropriate feelings on everyone else in the middle of dinner. She doesn't pick food off other people's plates, or grab uneaten leftovers out of the garbage, saying, "there's nothing wrong with this." But even my well-behaved sister-in-law couldn't ignore the murmurings. "I heard there's video?" she asked, as the two of us diced peppers for a salad. Perhaps she was trying to connect in the way women do while preparing a meal, with a sense of shared knowing. But at the time, the idea of my courteous sister-in-law venturing down this path sent me into a rage.

I slammed down the knife, stormed off and told the kids to pack their things. "We're leaving," I announced. My sister-in-law trailed me, immediately apologetic. I didn't listen. Just like in the immediate aftermath of Seth's suicide, I wanted to flee to a place where I could control the information, where I could choose to erase the image of the dark figure plummeting toward the ground, away from the "blunt trauma to the torso," described in his death certificate.

The girls gathered round.

"We can leave if that's what you really want," Sophia said. The two of them put their hands on my shoulders, one on each side. It was a sweet gesture, but I wriggled away, jerked open the car door and sat down hard in the driver's seat.

Julia walked around to my side and knocked on the window. Only her small head and curly hair were visible. "Mama," she said, "couldn't we just stay? It's family."

Her appeal was irresistible. I grumpily got out of the car and rejoined everyone for dinner. We all pretended nothing happened. But the video remained.

The following day I called Adam.

"Who has the video?" I asked. He told me if I really wanted it, he'd find out. Within an hour, my phone rang.

"It's been destroyed," he said. Standard procedure. That's what the state does with all of those endless hours of bridge footage, so much of it just heavy traffic and angry, sore-backed drivers trying to get home after a day. The tape is gone.

I exhaled, drank in that single moment of reprieve, knowing it would not last long.

Chapter 22

Vertigo

There's a particular type of vertigo that runs in my family. My mother, brother and I all suffer from variations of this ill-defined condition. We'll wake up in the morning, and even a slight torque of the head starts the world spinning. "I've got one of my dizzy spells," my mother will say, weakly, fumbling to keep the phone aligned to her ear, and I understand exactly what she's feeling. The disorder can be triggered by lack of sleep, greasy food, stress, or nothing at all. There is no warning.

After Seth died, my dizzy spells increased. When they were severe, I'd remain in bed, completely still, for hours. With minor bouts, I'd try to muscle through the day, just slightly off kilter. For me, grief had that same lurching, misaligned quality. I'd stagger from event to event, from work to dinner preparation, trying and failing to focus, my concentration fuzzy. Even when I'd try to unwind, with a friend at a bar on a Friday night, for instance, I'd often excuse myself to leave early, rushing home to bed. I couldn't gain traction anywhere, it seemed, and pretty much everything left me spinning with worry about my kids, ruminating about loss and shocked by my shitty luck.

My mother, once again, tried to help by offering a distraction, one of her "crumbs of pleasure." Now retired from her teaching job, she had a side gig as a volunteer usher at off-Broadway shows. Every Saturday or Sunday for decades, she'd pull on a pair of black slacks and a white button-down blouse and hop on the subway to work a matinee. She'd often phone me afterwards with a review, and her excitement spilled over to my children: for them, there was no special treat that topped a show in New York.

Before I had any clear sense of how to parent grieving children while grieving myself, I made many decisions based on a single criterion: Did it make us happy? Theatre always did.

When my mother treated us to tickets for the musical *Beautiful*, about the life of Carole King, I'm not sure Julia, then age 9, understood the nuances of the storyline, but she definitely got the gist. A Jewish girl from Brooklyn with a brilliant voice overcame adversity and a cad husband to become a feminist pop music icon. For me, Carole King was like family. Her hit record, *Tapestry*, still sits on a crowded shelf alongside the Streisand, Dylan, and Janis Ian albums in my mother's Brooklyn apartment. It was part of the soundtrack of my own 1970s childhood, a blur of divorce, Danskin, Marlo Thomas' *Free to Be You And Me*, and later, nickel bags on Myrtle Avenue, making out in denim overalls, and the smoking lounge at St. Ann's.

When Carole launched into, "Will You Still Love Me Tomorrow," I couldn't contain myself. Julia held me, saying, "Breathe, Mommy, breathe." The song spoke to my plight: The too-good-to-be-true pleasure of finding your person, the persistent dread that it can't possibly last. The fragility of hope. Carole got grief.

For months afterward, Julia and I would belt out our favorites in the car or over breakfast. "You've got to get up every morning with a smile on your face," she'd sing, directing her words to me, finger wagging, trying to make me smile. These songs, I realized, helped us metabolize our loss, churn it up and release it through our organs: heart, lungs, throat.

By the time I took the kids to see *Hamilton* to celebrate Sophia's 13th birthday, the kids had memorized all the lyrics, followed the cast members on Instagram and wore their "Young, Scrappy & Hungry"

T-shirts to special occasions. Julia said when she grew up she wanted to be an usher, so she could see *Hamilton* every day. Sophia dreamed of the future when high schools would gain access to the copyrighted material so she could get a part in the show—any part at all.

In the midtown Manhattan theatre, the lights dimmed, the opening rap started, and the girls froze. I'm not sure they breathed during that first number, and when it was over, they screamed and clapped, exuding the same blend of hysteria and rapture exhibited by those pony-tailed teenagers at The Beatles' first concert in America.

After Hamilton's son is killed in a duel, the heart tugging begins in earnest. We adopted "Living Through the Unimaginable" as our anthem, a road map through Griefland. "There are moments that the words don't reach, there is suffering too terrible to name, you hold your child as tight as you can and push away the unimaginable."

In the middle of the song, I peeked over and saw Sophia sniffling and wiping her eyes. She began sobbing uncontrollably. Even in the dark theater, I could see her big tears, her body shaking. It was the first time I'd seen her cry so deeply since Seth died. She couldn't stop, asked for one tissue, then another. The song had half the audience weepy, and my own chest tightened, too.

Still, I felt certain that, for Sophia, the sorrow suffused her on an almost cellular level. She'd held it together in school, never taking a day off, dutifully memorizing the capital cities of every African nation, completing all the bonus math work, and reading nonstop to keep the images of death from permeating her world. Maybe now, I thought, the physical pain she'd worked so hard to contain would find a way out through these scores, in the lyrics of someone else's tragedy. Sophia may have rejected our grief group and refused therapy. But she did have Lin-Manuel Miranda.

Chapter 23

Landmines

I was attuned to the landmines all around. Each passing mention of the word "suicide" tugged on the wound a little. I'd forgotten it was there—surprise!—in random movies we'd pick on a rainy afternoon (*Dead Poets Society*) and in the oblivious chatter of friends ("talk me off the ledge" or "just shoot me now").

"I want to watch *13 Reasons Why*," Sophia whined one day. "Everyone else is."

"No," I said, "It's scary and inappropriate."

"But it's not even real," she swung back at me, as if this fiction of suicide in no way related to our reality.

I didn't see then that my children were drawn to stories that faced death squarely, named it, but featured other families trapped in its grip. Somehow, I now understand, this took the burden off them. They could observe the mangled wreckage from the safety of the living room.

"It's just a *story*."

But while they relied on such stories to help them navigate death, I was repelled by fictional suicides and torn up families. They required even more of my vigilance. As a parent, I wasn't only grieving my own loss, but I was also compelled to manage the children's.

"There is a teen suicide in *Dear Evan Hansen*," my mother told me, but she thought Sophia and Julia would like the hip, *au courant* vibe of the musical, which quickly drew a cult following. What she didn't mention was that the entire plot hinges on a misinterpreted suicide note. This detail slowly revealed itself while I sat with the girls at the Music Box Theatre in New York during a school vacation. I felt certain that, at any moment, they would finally ask the question I dreaded: Did Dad leave a note? This thought distracted me throughout the play. My eyes kept darting over to them as I tried to gauge their reaction, and telepathically will their minds to stick with the story on stage.

I hadn't told the girls about Seth's note for many reasons, but one dominated: it hurt too much. His suicide may have been the inevitable outcome of illness, but he chose to do it. The note was proof of this choice.

I knew the note existed from the beginning. The state trooper had alerted me right after delivering the news of Seth's death. My cousin had taken the note and eventually it was passed to Adam, for safe keeping. Even though I couldn't bring myself to read it, I obsessed over its contents.

"Does it say anything I need to know?" I'd asked Adam that first summer. "Does it make sense, or is it just crazy, loopy words? Are there surprises?

"No, none of that," he'd said. "It's just sad."

It's odd looking back on this: I was simultaneously desperate to know and also, to not know. To understand from afar. Without the hard edge of confirmation.

Adam told me that other family members wanted to read the note too, but he was awaiting my approval. "No one else can read it," I'd said. "They won't understand." I wasn't interested in anyone else's interpretation of Seth's motives or their desire to make sense of his actions. That was my role alone. The note was an object left for me and my daughters to hold. It was personal, with the intimacy of a love letter and the finality of a fatal prognosis.

Evan Hansen was almost over, and I still had no plan. I would just have to muddle through, answer with words that I'd relied on earlier: *He loved you. It wasn't anyone's fault.*

When the show ended, the three of us stood up and cheered. They loved it. Together, both girls turned toward me. I braced myself. In unison, they asked, "Can we get the soundtrack, please?" I practically fell to the floor with relief. "Of course," I said, "let's buy it right now. We can memorize the words on the ride home."

Chapter 24

The Note

I'd been fearing it, pushing it aside for nearly nine months. Then, I simply grew weary of imagining. I had to read Seth's note.

Adam would be in town that raw, wet afternoon. He'd never missed a single performance of our family operas, always bringing the girls flowers and hosting a meal after the show. I'd told him I was ready, so that day, before heading back home to Connecticut, he stopped by our house to say one last goodbye. He pulled me aside and gestured to follow him upstairs, where he drew a sealed envelope from his jacket pocket and handed it to me. As if in a trance, I held the envelope and walked slowly into my bedroom. Suddenly drained of strength, I sat down on the edge of the bed. I trembled while unfolding the single sheet of paper.

I perceived the shape of the letters first: the blocky handwriting was fully recognizable. The sentences were short. The margins wide. There were no wild flourishes. I thought, if his brain went haywire, why was his grammar intact, with paragraph breaks, our names, and the date?

The pain of the note was simple: it was pure Seth. I imagined him that morning, sitting at his desk, choosing this lined paper, that black pen. There is so much I will never know, but I know he wrote these words:

I took Wellbutrin.

It gave me tinnitus.

The sound never, ever stops.

I've broken my brain.

I can't think. I can't sleep.

I can't be a husband or

Father or researcher or teacher.

I'm so sorry to hurt everyone like this.

Someday I hope you will forgive me.

Rachel, Sophia & Julia—I love you.

July 1, 2014.

My face flushed with the heat of tears. A sense of crumbling, the weight of these sentences, forced my head to bow down. I thought about Seth composing this note, composing himself to write it, wondering if the transgressive act of committing these words to this page might have been alarming enough that he'd considered stopping himself right then and there. Or did his plan become inevitable, the trigger itself, as he spelled it all out in terrible clarity?

I placed the note back in its envelope. Adam moved in closer and put his arms around me. "I know," he said. "I know."

Suddenly, a thought jolted me upright: *I must hide it.* Rushing out of my bedroom toward the back office closet, I tucked the envelope into an unmarked folder on a top shelf the children could not reach. For years, it remained concealed between a batch of old bank statements and unsorted junk mail.

I wouldn't read the note again for the better part of a year. And, after that, only rarely, when I wanted a surge of harsh remembrance. Each time I pulled it out, I saw a new facet: his desperation, the need for quick relief, a plea for our forgiveness. Every time, I felt my breath clutch, then a diffuse, stone-cold stillness. Time passed; the note stayed the same. We evolved, it was immutable.

Within it lived that original question: How can we go on?

What the note never offered is a true explanation of Seth's actions. He appeared to lay out an argument to justify his decision, but these were the words of a man consumed by his own hellish pain, possibly suffering from a flare-up of undiagnosed bipolar disorder he could not face. Rather than clarify his intentions, the note demanded further inquiry. Did the Wellbutrin really worsen his tinnitus? Or did his lack of sleep cause him to more fully fixate on the tinnitus? Did the one-and-a-half tablets of Seroquel prescribed by the psychiatrist unleash a surge of disinhibition? Did the chronic back pain or lack of exercise or the hard reality of turning 50 fuel a sense of shame too big to overcome? Did all of these elements contribute to an impulsive, very bad decision one summer morning?

My problem with Seth's note is that it didn't completely line up with the explanation of mental illness that I'd relied on to help the kids understand what had happened. I'd told them that his brain was "broken" due to a sickness and that it was this ailing organ that caused him to die. Just like a malfunctioning heart can kill you, I'd said, and a clump of renegade cells can drive a deadly cancer, so, too, this disease compelled him to death. It wasn't really a choice. But if this were true, where was the irrefutable evidence of his madness: the incoherent, grandiose language; the random capital letters? Could the note mean that, in fact, he did make a choice, the ultimate betrayal and abandonment? Or did he honestly believe he'd failed us and we were better off without him?

Chapter 25

Reading Between the Lines

My bedside table became a little library of grief as I continued my search for understanding. Kay Redfield Jamison, who wrote the definitive suicide book, *Night Falls Fast*, offered some wisdom: The final words of a suicide note are often banal, not delusional or loopy as one might imagine. "Suicide notes in general have a concrete, stereotypic quality to them," she wrote. "More concerned about the pain and suffering they knew would be caused by their acts; more neutral in tone [and] although more likely to express psychological pain, more likely [too] to use the word "love" in their texts."

When I called Jamison, I got the sense, even through her academic tone, that she wanted to make me feel better. She no doubt understood: A clinical psychologist who'd suffered from manic-depressive illness (now called bipolar disorder), Jamison had investigated her own wild mood swings and suicidality in her memoir, *An Unquiet Mind*. She explained to me that it's not just garden variety "unwell-ness" that typically leads to suicide, rather, it's a toxic brew of psychic pain and suffering overlaid on the particularities of a person's vulnerability. This includes a hard-wired sensibility attuned to shame, defeat, or failure when others might experience the same events as, simply, a tough patch to endure, even a challenge to rise above. In her book, Jamison makes this critical distinction: "Much of the decision to die is in the construing of events...People seem to be able to bear or tolerate depression as long as there is the belief that things will improve. If that belief cracks or disappears, suicide becomes the option of choice."

Suicide, historically, has been defined alternatively as a sin, a crime, and a manifestation of disease. The suicidologist Edwin Shneidman asserted that the key to understanding suicide is to acknowledge the sufferers' unique state of mental pain and anguish, something he called "psychache."

This made sense, and explained, in part, why it was so very difficult to place myself in Seth's shoes.

Still, I continued to seek out anyone who might offer a storyline I could live with.

One evening, I ran into Dan Brenner, a classmate from high school, whose son was in Julia's fifth grade class. I quickly struck up a conversation with him about suicide. Dan, a psychiatrist, gently suggested that it might be better to hold off, and chat about this topic after the 10-year-olds finished their performance on filial piety in ancient China. He invited me to his office to talk further. He didn't know Seth personally, but he knew about bipolar and depression and self-harm and had seen it up close in his practice treating severely ill patients. It took many months to schedule our meeting but I finally made it to his Cambridge office.

In our small world, where I was privileged to have access to doctors and lawyers and scholars who charged me nothing for their time because they just wanted to help, I found it amusing that he worked right across the hall from my own therapist. I noticed he was offering ketamine treatment to his patients, and thought that Seth would have liked the idea of a party drug to improve his mood. Dan was convincing as he told me what I desperately wanted to hear. "There are behaviors that look like choices that don't take into account how biologically determined they are," he said. "We overestimate the amount of stuff that's within our control."

It's possible, he said, that Seth was in some kind of dysregulated state in which a set of circuits in his brain were triggered and the pathway to suicide, at that point, was set. This had nothing to do with his feelings about me, or his love for the kids, or the state of our marriage: "It's like he got a GI virus, and then he vomited."

I leaned into Dan's words. With each statement, I experienced a flicker of possibility that maybe there really was nothing I could have done. "When dogs get sick they all act the same. They shake and cower and we don't say the dog is making a choice," Dan continued. "We do things that are programmed by our evolution, and sometimes that's very hard to explain."

This may have been the singularly lousy way Seth's illness unfolded. Another man might have, one day, announced he'd gambled away the house or had sex with other women. Self-harm is a known symptom of this disease. "It's not anyone's choice," Dan reiterated, speaking directly to my fear. "It's outside the realm of choice, like a fatal heart attack."

Seth never squarely acknowledged any recurring depression he'd had. People often said to me that it must have been so hard in our house, with Seth in so much pain for so many years.

Actually, no. His suicide was a shock, out of the blue. He was never diagnosed with a serious mental illness, there were no previous attempts. It's true that during his 20 years at MIT, he went to the mental health department complaining of feeling low, emotionally and physically, on a few occasions. Once, when he'd just arrived as a young assistant professor, in 1994, and had been through a particularly painful breakup. Again, when our kids were babies and no one in the house was sleeping, so we'd fight. Then, again, in November 2013, nine months before his suicide. Since I'd known him, the visits went pretty much the same way: He was prescribed an antidepressant and urged to pursue therapy. And on each occasion, he took the drugs for few weeks or maybe a month, reported that he felt better, and never followed up with therapy.

So, in late June of 2014, there was a nearly full bottle of Wellbutrin in our medicine cabinet. Seth didn't tell me at the time he was prescribed the drug, though I was aware of his various mid-life stressors. He also didn't tell me why he decided—two weeks before his death—to take a few Wellbutrin pills, and then stop after a couple of days.

I imagined at some point on the morning of July 1, Seth made a decision. Perhaps it was the moment after he kissed the girls goodbye and promised me that he'd remain on the couch reading *The Times* until I returned. Maybe it was when he watched the three of us bike off to camp. It's possible he'd been thinking about it for days, or years. I'll never know.

His note continues to reveal itself. The words sometimes appear like a vision, the block letters dancing before my eyes. Why did he use an ampersand, instead of the word "and" when he listed our names: Rachel, Sophia & Julia? Maybe, in his mind, we'd already fused into a single unit, a tight team of survivors. *Someday I hope you will forgive me*, he wrote. Most days, I can. He brought us death, but, also, so much life.

After years of living with the note-sadness lodged in my body, I came to see it in a new light. And I'd figured out what I'd eventually tell the children when they asked. The note was, in its own distorted way, an act of love. Seth sought to spare us whatever illness, broken-ness, less-than-Seth-ness he imagined he was becoming. He wanted to be the perfect dad, the masterful engineer, the beloved teacher, and unless he could be all of that—at the highest level—his life would fall short of the one he'd envisioned. He loved you so much, I would someday tell the girls, he just wanted flawless summer days and star-filled nights for the two of you, always. He hoped to create a dream world—and believed he could will it to come true.

Chapter 26

The Bridge

I have not been able to cross the Tobin Bridge since Seth's suicide. I don't know if I ever will. I came close on the first Easter Sunday we spent without him. We'd been invited to lunch at Adam's house in rural Connecticut. I had little interest, but the girls were so enthusiastic, I couldn't say no.

It might have been easier to distance myself from Seth's family. I'd sometimes wonder if they believed I'd failed to take care of him, faltered as a wife. No one has ever said that, nor even hinted at it. On the contrary, Seth's large, close-knit family—especially his parents and brothers—have always made it clear that they don't blame me in any way for Seth's actions. My in-laws are consistently gracious and generous and compassionate. They have conveyed, in action and words, that they will always love the girls and do anything for them; they consider me family, a daughter, and that will not change.

For this reason, and to retain a sense of order in my children's lives, I'd willed myself to lose the bad attitude and rise to an Easter visit. At least that's what I tried to do as we rolled past stables and open fields and the town's old-style gazebo. But when we arrived at the house, I realized I wasn't fully present. I couldn't look at the ham, barely smiled when the kids ran outside for sack races, and found I had zero patience for the barrage of polite questions. "How *are* the girls?" and "How are *you*?" I avoided the chitchat by locking myself in the bathroom to check and recheck my phone for no other reason than distraction. I quickly began planning our exit.

Once the egg hunt loot was sorted, and the girls' favorite ricotta cheesecake consumed, I eagerly directed them to say goodbye. My nephew had agreed to drive us back into town, which was lucky because it was dusk and I was exhausted and unsure about my reliability behind the wheel. Ben took the driver's seat and we settled in for the ride back to Tufts, where he was a student, and then home.

After about 90 minutes, the kids fell asleep and I dozed off briefly. But as my eyes fluttered open, I suddenly bolted to attention. We must have missed our exit, I thought, because we were headed toward the Tobin Bridge. "Fuck," I said to Ben. "We need to find another route." Confused, he turned to me. "The bridge," I explained, "it's the bridge, I don't want to go over it." Generally even-keeled, Ben suddenly seemed jittery.

"Where should I go?" he said. I hadn't a clue. My phone had died and I'd forgotten a charger. I was unclear about the route to Tufts, and, meanwhile I was certain we were approaching the bridge with no way out. Our commotion up front woke the girls.

"What's going on?" Sophia said.

"Nothing, just trying to figure out directions." I tried to sound nonchalant.

The Tobin Bridge sign loomed. My heart began to race, my mouth turned dry. I was not prepared to do this. I did not want to be in the same spot where Seth experienced his last moments, to see the precise height from which he fell. To be there accidentally, and with the girls, made it even worse. I had planned to someday stand dramatically atop the bridge and face this reckoning. At some future date, I'd be ready to feel the wind at that height, let my muscles inhabit its shaky danger, and imagine preparing for physical pain. But I wanted my first sense of the true terribleness of the bridge to be methodical, controlled, on my terms.

"We can't do this, you've got to go another way!" I raised my voice. This barreling toward the bridge was an element in recurring dreams, the sense that I was rushing toward a precipice with no brakes.

My nephew—poor kid—was hapless. He'd struggled in his own quiet way over the death of a favorite uncle who adored him. Together they'd invent knock-knock jokes and make each other crack up with outrageous pranks. At the funeral, Ben's father conceded that his kids were happier playing with Seth than with their own dad.

But none of that mattered now. I was hyper-focused on avoiding the bridge, as if it would suck us down, like it had done to Seth. It was a hulking monster, a widow-maker, an ugly Boston crossing that took Seth's life because it was too close to our home and too seductive for a distressed engineer who'd run out of options on a Tuesday morning in July.

"Just fucking exit," I finally yelled, thinking, yet again, that I might actually be having a heart attack. The kids were now fully awake and perplexed. Ben was doing his best to find a way out, trying to project a calm exterior, like his side of the family usually did. My screaming and cursing didn't help. Then, I spotted a familiar exit. I reached over to grab the wheel, then reconsidered, pulled my arms back and barked: "Turn. Here. Now."

The car swerved toward the off-ramp. This unbalanced swing in space sent me back in time, to when the state trooper confirmed Seth was dead. My first instinct was to latch on to what I considered to be the most plausible explanation. I thought he was in a car accident; that Seth had, in a confused state, crashed on Memorial Drive along the river. To me, this made far more sense than suicide.

Years before, he'd been working with students to perfect a self-driving car. He was smitten with this project; a vision of the future. But the results were mixed. Talos, the Land Rover that his team commandeered, came in fourth place in the big national competition. This wasn't too bad considering the many ways the vehicle stumbled and swerved on the course, a dusty Army base set up to resemble a city, in Southern California. As part of the contest, Talos faced the challenges of driving in any urban center; navigating among other moving vehicles, rerouting around roadblocks, quirky local rules of the road. Maneuvering in this manner, Seth wrote later, required "algorithms doing reasonable and not-so-reasonable things," because, of course, no one was behind the wheel.

Maybe, I thought on the day of his death, no one was behind that wheel either. Maybe he smoked a joint and got a little reckless, or reached down to change the radio station, shifting his focus just long enough to lose control. Maybe he called a student to join him on a joy ride in one of his sensor-laden autonomous vehicles, and this geeked-out-bad-boy romp spun out of control, into a guardrail, plunging down toward the water.

My imagination was simply not expansive enough to conjure him jumping off a bridge. Though I'd long been a catastrophizer, often fearing the worst, this went too far, even for me.

Days later, when I knew for sure it wasn't an accident, when I found his cell phone under his pillow in the bed I now slept in alone, the word "accident" still reverberated through my mind. The true cause just didn't match with our lives. I wanted it to be an accident so badly. People have car accidents. An accident would have been far easier to manage; so much simpler to accept.

But in this moment, I now saw, my nephew had navigated us out of danger. Deposited into Charlestown, we passed Bunker Hill Community College and headed toward the river, the mall, and the familiarity of my neighborhood. Sensation returned to my limbs, and my breathing began to deepen. By this time, it was dark. Our detour would extend an already long day. But that was fine. We'd avoided the bridge, for now.

Chapter 27

Out of Control

Fearing the worst had long been my default. So, when the worst actually happened, that familiar tread of worry deepened even further. Widowhood simply magnified my unease, gave it power. My control freakishness blossomed, now fueled by a sense that life owed me something because of what I'd lost. The more out-of-control things felt, the harder I fought back. I dropped Sophia off for a month of sleepaway camp when she was 12, and, by that time, I'd become a kind of caricature of motherhood.

I already knew that at this woodsy, all-girls camp in the Berkshires, kids were not permitted to call home, only to write letters sent through the U.S. mail. How would I monitor Sophia's mood and stability? What if she plummeted and none of the teenage counselors noticed? Weeks before the session started, I'd engaged in a lengthy discussion with the camp director, explaining Seth's suicide and my concerns. I needed to hear my daughter's voice periodically, I'd said. Also, to ensure her mental health, I insisted she be placed in a cabin with two close friends from school, Rosie and Esme.

"It's only been one year," I told the director. "She needs support, her friends. What if something goes wrong?" The director was deeply understanding, but also gave the impression that she'd dealt with highly demanding mothers many times before. Still, we agreed that given the circumstances, it would be acceptable to break the no-calling-home policy and allow me a weekly check-in.

When we arrived at camp on a muggy Sunday afternoon, I learned that Sophia had been assigned to a cabin without her friends. As the kind, young—and clearly oblivious—counselor began explaining that it was healthy for kids to meet new people, I cut her off mid-sentence and demanded a supervisor. "I was promised she'd be with her friends," I said, marching off to find an adult to fix my problem.

"Please, Mom, it's fine," Sophia said. "I'll just stay in this cabin."

"No, actually, you won't."

I didn't relax until I found a sympathetic administrator who approved my request. Triumphant, I lugged Sophia's duffel bag and bedding to her new, proper cabin and made up the bunk bed. I couldn't bring Seth back for my daughter, but at least I could insulate her with familiar bunkmates and blankets. She glared as I fluffed the pillow we'd brought from home.

"There," I said, smugly. "That's better."

My unending maternal power grab was exhausting. When the counselors gently told the parents it was time to go, I walked hesitantly to my car and crumpled into the driver's seat. Even with my success in re-orchestrating the cabins, I was anxious about leaving Sophia on her own. But I had no choice. Heading to the turnpike, I cranked up "We Are Young," opened all the windows, and sped toward my next project— Julia—awaiting me in Cambridge. About an hour into the drive, my phone rang and I saw the 413 area code: a call from camp. My heart accelerated so uncontrollably that I had to pull over.

"Is everything okay?" I said, pressing my mouth into the phone as if that might get me closer to the news.

"Hi," said a young voice. "Is this Sophia's mom? I'm one of her counselors."

Before she could even speak, my mind raced to a conclusion. *Oh my God, something happened already?* I knew I never should have left. Immediately, I re-started the car, jerked the steering wheel to the far left, preparing to make a quick U-turn. I could fix this, I thought, return to camp, collect my daughter, and bring her home where she belonged. What was I thinking, sending her away? This familiar script ensnared me; every time I relaxed my guard, terrible things happened.

"Everything's fine," the counselor said. "I just wanted to call and tell you Sophia aced her swim test and now she's just hanging out with her friends in the cabin. She's doing great." I stopped the car again, releasing my grip from the wheel.

"Thank you. Thank you so much," I said.

As soon as I arrived home, I began counting the days until our weekly check-in call. When the time came, I settled into my bedroom with the door shut tight. I dialed. When I heard Sophia's distant voice on the line, I yearned to touch her face, tuck her loose hair behind her ears and scoop her into my arms. "I'm fine," she said, unconvincingly. And then she wasn't. Her voice grew shakier, uneven, until finally, she began to cry. "I miss you," she said. "I miss home."

Again, I was up and ready to drive the two-and-a-half hours to pick her up. "I'm coming for you," I said. "It's okay. I'm leaving now." A counselor then joined us on the line. "You know, she really was doing great until she spoke to you. This is completely normal for new campers. Why don't we give it a couple more days?"

This counselor, and then another one, tried to calm me down. And somehow, they convinced me to stay still, sit with all of this for a day. During that 24-hour period, I must have called a dozen professionals and therapeutically-savvy friends to try to determine if Sophia's sadness was "normal" homesickness, or pathology. Were her genetic ties to Seth instigating a slippery slope toward destruction? I could not let this happen again.

In the end she stuck it out. So did I.

When I visited three weeks later for "Moms' Weekend" Sophia silently led me toward a clearing in the woods near a slow-moving river, to the camp's weekly Sunday morning gathering. It was clear and crisp, and all of the adults sat in a semi-circle on stone benches, amidst the campers dressed for the occasion in flowered skirts and paisley tops, and fuzzy, mismatched socks under their Birkenstocks. Alone, or in small clusters, the campers took to the makeshift stage to recite poems about the power of girlhood and finding the strength to resist peer pressure. When it was Sophia's turn, she stood and faced the crowd. Taking a deliberate breath, she wrapped both hands around the mic, like in prayer, and began to sing.

I knew I would cry, but I thought I could control myself. I was wrong. I wept chaotically, excessively, as my friend Hilary moved toward me on one side, my friend Sarah on the other, clutching my quivering shoulders, stroking my hair. Clearly it was *me* who needed my girlfriends at camp. Another mother in the crowd turned around to take in the scene unfolding behind her. Why was a grown woman losing it over a 12-year-old singing a Colbie Caillat ballad about honoring your inner beauty? This other woman wondered if, perhaps, there was more to the story then she knew. Had she asked, I would have told her: I cried because my daughter survived. I cried because her father went missing. I cried because I'd lost control and there was no gaining it back.

Chapter 28

Leonard

I'd been searching for "Leonard" for several years. Not Leonard, exactly, but a man with Leonard's life story—or, more precisely, his near-death story. Leonard, I learned, jumped off the same bridge as my husband. The difference is that Leonard lived.

I wanted to meet Leonard because I thought he might answer some of the questions I'd never be able to ask Seth: What were you thinking when you stepped off the ledge? Were you scared? Did it hurt? In those last moments, did you consider the people who loved you? The destruction you'd leave behind?

Once, shortly after Seth died, a friend with cancer, exploring the contours of death as her own came closer, asked if I wanted to meet with a medium who channels the dead. Even though I am a thoroughly un-mystical person, I was intrigued, and considered her offer. When you lose someone too soon, that's what you want: One last word with your dead person, a moment to convey your final thoughts, to set the record straight. I came close to saying yes, envisioning an ecstatic reunion with the man I'd loved and lost. But then I thought pragmatically about what I'd honestly say to Seth if we did talk, and realized I might lose it.

Me: What the fuck were you thinking leaving two little girls without a father?

Him: I'm sorry.

Me: You don't abandon your family like that. You get help, you act like a grownup.

Him: It was the best option at the time.

Me: Really? I don't think so. You made a promise when you had kids.

Him: You're better off without me.

Me: No, we're not. You should have stayed.

In other words, I thought there was an excellent chance that I would not be able to conjure up kindness or loving forgiveness in that dark chamber, one I imagined filled with stifling air thick with patchouli incense and sage-scented candles. Ghost Seth and I could very possibly have a major fight as the medium shrank behind her fringed scarves, thinking, perhaps, that he jumped because he married such a pain in the ass.

Would I lose it with Leonard, too? I hoped not. I was pretty sure that I could summon up my best behavior. After all, I wanted something from Leonard, something intimate; his story, mapped onto mine.

I had heard about a Leonard-like character just hours after Seth died. On that day, when I knew I would need a script to follow so I could tell the children what had happened, Dr. Paula Rauch, the expert I spoke with, came to the rescue. She had helped me find the words that might allow me to hold it together while conveying the worst possible news to my girls. Once that was settled, I allowed other random fears to bubble up, letting loose on the phone with a barrage of anxious questions about my uncertain future.

Me: Will my kids be permanently damaged?

Dr. R.: No, you can survive this, they can too.

Me: Can you literally die from a broken heart?

Dr. R.: Again, no, but you have to take care of yourself.

Me: Will I ever have sex again?

Dr. R.: Yes, if that's what you want. Give it time. Start with something casual.

Me: The plumber?

Dr. R.: Something like that…

Rauch's answers were direct and insightful. She seemed unflappable in the face of my acute trepidation. So I continued my line of questioning. "Have any of your patients ever done this?" I asked. I knew of no one else who'd ever jumped off a bridge; it seemed like such an outlandish, reckless act.

Rauch told me that none of her patients had died this way, but that one of her colleagues had attempted suicide by throwing himself off the Tobin years ago while he was still in medical school. He survived, and now practiced medicine in town, she said. I wanted more, but she wouldn't disclose his name or further details. From that moment, I felt a need to find this man. I thought he could help me understand Seth's compulsion to reject what appeared to be a charmed life. Over the years I would ask around, trying to find this doctor-survivor, but despite my probing, his identity remained secret.

Then, while discussing with a writer friend my search for the jumper who lived, she startled. "I know a guy who survived a suicide attempt off the Tobin Bridge," she said. This man was not the doctor I'd been looking for, but another guy—a man called Leonard.

After my friend secured permission and contact information, I texted Leonard, explaining that I was a journalist, working on a book about my husband's suicide and hoping to speak with him about his own experience. Leonard's response was curt. "Let's do this," he wrote.

We planned to get together the following week. I suggested one of the cafes on Massachusetts Avenue in Central Square, the slightly more gritty, urban section of Cambridge. "How about the 1369 Coffee House, or the Starbucks on Prospect Street," I wrote.

"How's Au Bon Pain in Central?" he wrote back.

On the day we were to meet, my nerves were on edge from the moment I woke up. I wondered whether my scheme to interview Leonard was ill-considered. Would it leave me even more troubled and sad for what might have been? Or worse, angry at an innocent, unsuspecting man because he lived and my husband did not?

When I entered the cafe, I quickly approached the first man I saw. He was swarthy, middle-aged and with a headful of dark hair—he looked a lot like Seth. My palms became clammy.

"Leonard?" I asked.

"No," he said politely.

I scanned the room more carefully, and spotted an older man with mottled skin, gray hair, and a ragged expression. Sitting at a table tucked in the back corner, Leonard's solid frame slouched heavily in his chair as if he'd been there for some time. He held a paper cup of coffee in one hand, and looked his age, which was 70. I sized him up: furrowed brow, scruffy beard, a bit of Mandy Patinkin (circa *Homeland*, not *Criminal Minds*) but paler. Someone who'd easily recede into a crowd.

We locked eyes and I approached him. As I took the seat opposite Leonard, I noticed that the table was oddly misaligned and wobbled slightly as I leaned on it. If Seth were here, I thought, he'd find a scrap of cardboard, sink down to his knees and balance the chrome legs.

Drawing a deep breath, I launched into my memories of the immediate aftermath of Seth's death. I found myself surprisingly comfortable with this stranger, like he'd understand in a way that few others would.

"It felt like his suicide came out of nowhere," I said. "The worst was telling my girls. But it's been a few years now, and, you know, kids absorb things differently—they're actually okay, or, at least I think they are. You never really know, it could get bad at any moment." I thought if I dumped intimacies on the table, he'd return his own to me.

"That's tough for the kids," Leonard responded, sheepishly. "I'm sorry."

It struck me as odd that Leonard reacted the way most everyone else did to my story: a sympathetic shake of the head, a tinge of discomfort, the conventions of sympathy and a sense of disbelief. I thought his response would be different, that he'd offer insight, the wisdom of a parallel life. But I was here to lure details out of him, so I pressed record on my phone and asked Leonard to tell me his story.

On a Friday in June, 1984, Leonard woke up in the early afternoon. He showered, made coffee, and, just like that, decided to follow through "with the plan."

"It was a done deal," he said. "I wrote a suicide note, and then had no more thoughts about it. That day it was clear to me that that was the rational thing to do."

Leonard was 36 years old at the time, single, on the verge of homelessness and drinking heavily. Shortly after midnight, eight hours into his shift driving a cab, he said: "I just found myself sitting on the very top of the Tobin Bridge."

As Leonard spoke, I began a cold tally of the differences between Seth and the world-weary man sitting across the table. Leonard faced addiction and loneliness. He had no home or children. Seth appeared to have it all—two daughters, a dream job, and a wife who brought dancing and singing and a dark-witted warmth to his world. Leonard wanted out from a life of isolation, it appeared, while Seth turned his back on the domestic fantasy we'd built together. *Leonard's story was not our story*, I thought, unaware until much later that, in fact, it was. At the time, I had one prevailing question: Why did Seth die while Leonard lived?

"I sat there, about 190 feet up, for a couple of minutes," Leonard continued. "I took a few breaths, and then, I jumped."

At that moment, I retreated into my own reverie: The dream of another path. What if I had returned home to Seth just 15 minutes sooner—the time it took to buy my morning coffee? I might have biked up to our driveway and arrived just as Seth locked the front door and turned toward his car. He would have seen me, and maybe flashed back to the woman he fell in love with years before, an ambitious reporter with luxurious long hair. That morning I'd hastily pulled on an outfit: a sporty striped miniskirt and a vintage cotton camisole, low-cut and airy. Maybe Seth would have noticed my smooth shoulders and remembered how much we wanted each other back then, when we lived in distant cities and constantly imagined ways to be together, bare-limbed, arms intertwined with desire. "The kids are happy at camp," I might have said. "Where are you going?"

And Seth, momentarily distracted by my voice, the curve of my hips, may have been caught off guard just long enough to reconsider his plan. He'd walk toward me, reach for my hand, and confess, "It's not getting better. I'm scared." At that moment I'd drop my bike and lead him into the house.

"Come with me," I'd say. "You need to eat."

I'd fry him an egg in butter and slather strawberry jam on toast and we'd sit together while he drank a big glass of milk between sobs. These simple tastes, cream, sweet, salt, familiar like childhood, would ground him. And I would speak softly, patiently, without a hint of irritation, and tell him there is still so much good here, with us and his work and the children, who viewed him as a hero even with no heroics. Together we might have figured out a plan for him to take a break, even the whole summer off—Atlas, the robot, would be fine. Then I'd clear the dishes and walk him upstairs to our bed. I would notice his phone under the pillow, and wonder, briefly, why. But no matter. I'd tell him to lay on his belly so I could rub his shoulders. Perhaps, sensing some relief as the noise in his head subsided, Seth might have sighed audibly and splay his arms wide, allowing the pressure of my touch to ease away the hard knots. With his eyes closed, and his breath easy and regular, he'd fall into the safety of a deep sleep. I would remain there with him, my hands still on his warm skin, whispering, "You're okay, I am here."

But that was not how it unfolded. When I biked up to the house that morning, coffee in hand, Seth's car was already gone.

I snapped back and continued to pepper Leonard with questions. What were you feeling in those last moments? Can you remember your final thoughts? Did you imagine your mother? Could anyone have changed your mind? His answers remained the same. "There were no last thoughts, it was too dark a place to be," Leonard said. "You just shut down." And it hit me. Seth was not thinking of us when he jumped. He wasn't thinking at all.

On some level, I understood this tunnel vision. It had clouded my own thinking at times, as a teenager, stoned, up all night, making out with greasy-haired guys I didn't even like on fire escapes in Brooklyn. Or abroad at 16, lonely, homesick, yearning for connection, stealing Nutella and Toblerone bars from the corner store, eating cane sugar straight from the bag to dull the emptiness, the yearning to be someplace—anyplace—else. After college, speeding, wasted, from downtown San Francisco to Shrader and Waller with the busboy I was hooking up with. I understood the abandonment of reason, the aggravated hurt you want to extinguish with drugs or sex or pushing past the bounds of safety. But this comparison only went so far: In all my grasping for unconsciousness, I never considered crossing the threshold into complete oblivion.

And then, years later, children and motherhood suppressed what was left of my recklessness. Kids made me think twice about risk and responsibility. Sitting there with Leonard, I realized, flatly, that one difference between Seth and me was the clarity of purpose I gained as a mother.

But Seth, in his dark loop of pain, just couldn't spot a lifeline. It wasn't weakness, or lack of will, I saw now; it was his impetuous, black-and-white problem-solving. His left brain had tried desperately to find a rational solution to his immediate suffering. He'd made a terrible decision, but to him it made sense in the moment: This would stop the agony. Now. Forever. There's a "blind necessity" to ending such torment, the author William Styron wrote during his years struggling with depression. Seth suffered from a similar kind of blindness. In that moment, he didn't see himself as making a choice. He felt he had no other options.

In that instant, at the wobbly table, I began to understand a little more. I still think Seth might have been saved if the timing of events had aligned differently, and with the right kind of help. Yet I also glimpsed his distorted perspective: He must have felt he'd found a fix that would end his suffering and protect us from it, too.

This reckoning began a cascade of softening throughout my body. A slim film of forgiveness started to take hold. Seth had fought so hard, for so many years, to be the model father, the caretaker, the provider, the brilliance and the light in our home. Then, I suppose, he just couldn't manage the façade any longer.

Leonard was driven by a desperate desire to snuff out torment and find fast relief, a compulsion born of just the wrong blend of biology, circumstance, and opportunity. His life was likely spared because of a single contact he made just before jumping. He phoned the dispatcher on duty at the cab company that night and offered a heads up: "Tell the owner his cab is on top of the Tobin Bridge. He might want to call for a tow," Leonard had said. "I'm going over, I'll catch you later." The dispatcher immediately called 911.

Leonard tried to explain that moment to me. "You're not in your right mind," he said. He told me that he felt no pain as he fell from the bridge: "I blacked out immediately." That notion cast an unexpected calm my way. Someday, I thought, when my kids asked for details, I could say it didn't hurt, and I'd have proof, which offered some consolation.

There on the ledge, at the end, both Leonard and Seth thought of nothing else beyond escaping their intolerable distress; both thought the world would be better off if they were gone. "I didn't see any way out," Leonard said. "That wasn't true, but that was my reaction to what I perceived as my reality."

Leonard should not have survived. He told me he lost consciousness as he fell through the air at 80 mph. Miraculously, his body surfaced in the Mystic River just as state police arrived on the scene, having received the urgent call from the cab dispatcher. Harbor patrol showed up and fished Leonard from the water. He was rushed to Massachusetts General Hospital, where an ER doctor repaired his ruptured spleen and collapsed lung and multiple broken ribs.

Several days later, when he woke up with four-point restraints and sutures down his chest, Leonard was angry: he'd screwed up his own death. "I failed to do the job," he told me. "The odds of surviving are about 1 in 500. I felt like a failure in my attempt." He took a sip of his coffee and then lifted his eyes toward me.

Leonard had sincerely wanted it all to stop. His life had shriveled. "I was just going through the motions like a robot."

Hearing the word "robot" aloud shook me. Seth's robot, Atlas, had become a major presence in our lives. The robot had earned a de facto spot as a member of the family, like Seth's mercurial, stubborn, adolescent twin. Only bulkier. Sometimes, after supper, Seth would take the girls over to the hangar where his graduate students lovingly coaxed Atlas to walk up steps, get into a car, raise an arm. My kids would rush home with stories. "Atlas made it to the top step!" they'd shout, or sometimes, crushed, "Atlas fell down." After Seth died, the children periodically asked me how Atlas was feeling. "Is he sad?" they wondered. "Will he be okay?"

The pressure Seth placed upon himself to win a contest in which the rules kept changing was unfathomable and unrelenting. After constantly telling friends and family about Atlas's daring, audacious feats, had Seth known there was a chance his team might lose? What would everyone think? He was so driven to prove himself, to show, at the age of 50, that he'd lived a worthy life. Loss was, in his mind, unacceptable.

That sense of failure, I believe, began a kind of existential panic in Seth that led him to reach for the leftover medication in the medicine chest which disrupted his sleep, exacerbated the ringing in his ears, and left him vulnerable when the next wave of depression hit.

Leonard described his own long slog through recovery, getting clean, the work of "internal transformation." There were years of therapy and basement meetings, recalcitrance and rage, tightly embracing his 12-step blueprint, which turned out, he said, to be life-altering. As he spoke, I considered how Seth's alternate path might have looked: trips to some psychiatric facility in the suburbs, a leave of absence from work, the plummeting of status and ego.

Could Seth have asked for help, become more like Leonard with his Big Book, and pivoted toward quieter jobs, advocating for others with mental illness, recognizing himself in their struggles? Would Seth have accepted this lower-gloss reality? Less gleaming robot, more vulnerable human?

I knew Seth wasn't one to accept a "less than" scenario. He'd bolted on other occasions when life fell short of his expectations. Once, when the children were tiny, he ran out of the house with an overnight bag in a snowstorm because he didn't like my "tone." In bare feet, I chased him down the street, terrified to be left alone with two babies in the house, pleading for his return. But I viewed these lapses as flukes, one-offs. I married Seth precisely because he *was* so solid and reliable. The fixer. I loved him, in part, because he was so different from my other, less dependable boyfriends: the chain smoker with the black Mustang, the pasty British art dealer, the guy who actually preferred men, or the one who made me huckleberry muffins but also liked strippers.

As Leonard described his unwanted rescue, I looked straight into his tired eyes and saw a singularly brave man. His physical wounds healed after a few months, but he endured years of psychic hell, long stretches hunting for "self-realization." Dogged by financial uncertainty, filling out endless government forms for subsidized housing, Leonard would often wonder, "What's the point?"

Gradually, though, Leonard began to live again. He deepened his study of addiction and trauma, rediscovered his guitar, and began playing with musician friends. Recently, Leonard had started dating someone new. The pull toward death became an ancient memory. When he crossed the Tobin Bridge these days, Leonard sometimes slipped into a brief moment of reflection, but then snapped back to this life.

With our coffee cups emptied, Leonard and I shook hands and wished each other well. I walked into the grey, overcast afternoon harboring a hope that things with his girlfriend would continue to work out. In my parked car, I slumped into the driver's seat, drained and a little disappointed. Leonard had given me insight into the all-consuming grip of hopelessness, but he hadn't presented the "Aha" I was after. That big revelation opening up the mystery of Seth's death never materialized. Leonard only made me realize how capricious life can be, and how the answers I craved would never be complete, tidy, revelatory.

I had always believed in questions: that if I asked the *right* person the *right* question all would be clarified. In fact, this was not so. If Leonard proved anything, it was that talking to the right person only led to more questions. Those questions continued to emerge whenever I stumbled across bits of Seth: that final text message; a beat-up frisbee; an unsent wedding invitation we kept to show our kids; or, deep in an old jacket pocket, a bag of sea glass and shells he collected with the girls, which I imagine they might have transformed into an object of beauty, a necklace on a simple string, or a collage of treasures once hidden deep below the waves.

I started thinking of the other "Leonard," the doctor I'd heard about who survived the jump from the bridge, the one I hadn't yet found. Maybe I'd track him down someday, and he would unlock the secret. Or maybe, like this Leonard, he would reveal the limits of my inquiry, and instead show me how we stumble forward, through our chaotic, shimmering lives.

PART III

Chapter 29

To the Rescue

If pressed to rank the things that saved me, high up on the list would be my girlfriends, the Greek chorus of women whose love and dedication to my cause was unconditional.

Surprisingly, though, it wasn't always the people I expected who moved in close, ready to take on the mess of my world. I thought I knew who would stand like a rock of support, and who'd crumble. I was wrong. My close work colleague, for instance, a woman I shared intimacies with daily, approached me a few months after Seth's death and said she couldn't handle my relentless pain anymore. She bluntly told me to stop dumping my widowed-mom angst on her. We should talk about work, she said, that's it. Her rejection stung.

In similar ways, I imagined that an old friend of Seth's, a professor whose wife had suddenly died of a heart attack when their daughters were very young, might become a go-to guy for me. He and Seth used to take the kids on a dad-and-daughter camping trip every August; they'd defiantly eat non-organic hot dogs and pre-sweetened oatmeal from packets and return home covered with insect bites and smelling like smoke. Of all people, I thought this man would relate to the unforeseen loss of a spouse and its tumultuous aftermath. But when I reached out to him, there was no response. I later suspected that the paradox of Seth's suicide was too confounding: This guy would have done anything to keep his wife alive, and here, his friend ended his own life. It was probably just too much.

My own thinking veered in directions I'm now ashamed to admit. I ruthlessly began comparing deaths, envious of fatal cancers, for instance, because they were clear cut, with no one to blame. You could explain colon cancer to a child. Suicide was different, infused as it was with irrationality and shame. When I learned that a friend's elderly mother died peacefully in her sleep, I quietly fumed. I knew I should have responded with sympathy, but instead I felt jealous. "It was a beautiful death," this friend wrote in a group email, describing a series of beatific last moments; brushing her mother's hair, holding her hand, surrounded by family in the country home she grew up in, love all around. I so envied this "good death."

I wanted that in my life too. *How*, I stewed, *did I find myself so thoroughly screwed in the death department? Why didn't we get to say goodbye to Seth, touch his face?* My petty scoring of other deaths sometimes worked in reverse: Once in a while, someone else had it worse, and this, admittedly, made me feel better. At a party, I bumped into an acquaintance who'd lost her husband years ago. A heart attack, I'd been told. But after a few drinks, she said: "At least that's the story."

"Not a heart attack?" I said.

No, she shook her head. And because of my loss, and the particular awfulness of it, I was socially permitted to probe further. "What, then?"

She leaned over to whisper in my ear. She'd not shared this information with her adult children.

"Auto-erotic strangulation," she said.

I was certain I'd misheard her, so I asked her to repeat it.

"Wow," I said aloud. And then to myself: *That is definitely worse.*

My juvenile behavior was all unseen, so it didn't deter those committed to helping me. Women who had merely been in my social periphery took on central roles in the Mom Brigade. Kira raised money to replace my broken laptop, bought me massages and arranged meal deliveries to my door. Annkatrine picked Julia up for a weekly dance class with friends and then dropped her off at home. And Maria became my unshakeable partner, spending afternoons with the girls at the library or the playground or watching ducks by the river, allowing me time to work and think.

Maria had been caring for Sophia since she was two, and for Julia since birth. In that time, I'd never once heard her raise her voice or lose her temper or say "no" to any game or art project the kids asked for. "They are so beautiful," she'd tell me often. "You are lucky." Years later, when I drafted my will—neither Seth nor I had one, why would we?—I became stuck on the question of who might take the girls if I died. I approached Sophia. "Honey, nothing's going to happen to me, but if it ever did, who would you want to live with? Uncle Paul, Uncle Adam, Uncle David? What do you think?" She paused for a quick moment, looked straight at me, and replied: "Maria."

So many other women took turns driving the kids to and from school and birthday parties and events when I couldn't be in two places at once. Before Seth died, I was self-reliant, never the one whose kid always needed a ride. Now, I was *that* mom. But my resistance began to fall away as these women advanced, stepping over the line from mere kindness to first responders, rescuing me daily from my raging neediness. They brought fresh salads with beans and legumes and hummus, worried about my protein intake. Amy always picked up the phone at night, listening uncritically to every articulated fear I threw out no matter how insignificant or self-absorbed. Would I be single forever? How could I get to my favorite Sunday morning yoga class? After these calls, I would experience a sense of safety, being held, a connection that comes from gratitude, a form of relief I hadn't expected.

My friend Annie offered something different. A doctor who'd grown frustrated with the limitations of the U.S. health care system, she'd started a nonprofit to highlight the stories of people in the throes of serious illness, trauma, loss. She began recording and editing these stories, and eventually, we would launch a series called "Listening to Patients" that ran on our public radio health blog.

Annie approached me during that first summer and asked if I wanted her to record my story. I'd been so impressed by her view of storytelling as a key aspect of health care. She believed that the bottom-line rush of modern medicine had crushed humanity and compassion from the system. Stories, she argued, could bring those human elements back, and support healing. Back then, I didn't think that taping my story would offer any kind of catharsis or mending. I only knew that I wanted to remember the details for the future. Since both our daughters were already taking piano lessons at Annie's house once a week, we decided to find a quiet room while they were busy and start taping. We called this endeavor "The Piano Sessions."

I didn't know then what these sessions would become, but I did know that within days of Seth's death, a story, external to me, but also part of me, began to form in my mind. I even had a working title, *Off the Tobin Bridge: A Love Story*, a rom-com with a tragic twist. That's how my brain worked, evaluating every experience for its story potential, a kind of Nora Ephron, "everything is copy" approach to life. A fight became a dance, or at least a punchline in a story told over martinis and salted almonds. My health blog only codified this instinct to constantly spin my life into narrative.

When I listened to those first taped sessions later, I grew sad just hearing the sound of my own raspy voice. The words spilled out with a raw, guttural quality. And the sentences rambled, filled with asides and unfinished phrases. A storyline with no clue where it was going.

Annie and I met weekly through that entire first school year. She asked me leading questions and gently steered the conversation back into focus when I meandered too far afield. But mostly I just lurched from topic to topic, trying, unwittingly, to find meaning in my own words.

In early November, the first Thursday after Halloween, I sat in a chair by the window, and launched into the week's story.

Halloween was always Seth's domain, and I knew it would be

impossible for me to live up to the kids' very high expectations. I'd been trying to take on all of "his" activities with little success. He used to play a game with the girls called "Big Bed" which involved throwing them high up toward the ceiling in our bedroom. They'd land on the bed, and then hold positions I might call awkward, but they found funny. I hated this game. I worried they'd miss the bed and crash headfirst into the ground, or else hit a corner of the headboard and end up with a concussion. I'd dutifully played with them once, maybe twice, because I knew how much they loved it, but my effort was clearly half-hearted. I felt like the Viennese Baroness Schraeder in *The Sound of Music*, trying to ingratiate herself to the children by playing catch, when it was obvious she had nothing but disdain for these sorts of games. This was my state of mind approaching Halloween.

Summoning uncharacteristic gusto, though, I threw myself into the creation of a ghoulish tableau in our front yard. I'd enlisted the kids, and together we'd hoisted an oversized black, fuzzy spider to the top of the tetherball pole and fixed a strobe light to pulse directly on it. We arranged a headless mummy in a lawn chair playing poker with glow-in-the-dark aliens and a fortune-telling ghost. "Ta-da," I'd said, gesturing to a black cauldron of dry ice with its billowing smoke on our front stoop.

The girls were incredulous. "Nice, mom. How'd you do that?"

Feeling very Seth-like, I told them it was easy. I could see they were impressed, shocked, even, that I was able to rise to their father's level of Halloween theatricality. "See," I said, pouring water over the dry ice to thicken the steam plume. "We can do this."

Soon the streams of neighborhood children began arriving, and as I sat on the front steps handing out Hershey's kisses and mini packs of M&Ms, I remembered an early hint of Seth's tenderness. It was Halloween, 2000, and I was in my Brooklyn apartment on the phone with him while he sat at the very spot I was in now greeting trick-or-treaters. "You're so beautiful," he'd say to the little girl in the rhinestone tiara and bubble-gum pink gown walking towards him on the stone path. "You're the most beautiful princess ever."

I knew he was speaking to the kid, but I heard his words traveling towards me through the phone line. Again and again that night, even in our different cities, the words he repeated, "You're so, so beautiful," wove a kind of web between us, something real I could fall into with confidence.

As I concluded the day's recording with Annie, I felt a kernel of accomplishment. So often, I failed to be the girls' mother and father simultaneously. So often I felt that I'd let them down, choosing pragmatism over adventure, productivity over play. But with our cauldron bubbling, for one night at least, I was able to pull it off. This sense of a happy ending surprised me. I had momentarily suspended my obsession with deciphering Seth's story. I knew that to survive, I'd have to figure out my own.

Chapter 30

A Potential Guy

The email from a friend arrived unexpectedly, just as another brutal New England winter began its thaw. "Hi there," she wrote, "do you have a minute for a quick call about a potential guy?" I perked up, surprised by a long-forgotten twinge of romantic sizzle. On the phone, she mentioned his intelligence and kindness. He was divorced, with a daughter. There was, of course, a catch: He teaches at MIT, she told me. "Is that a deal-breaker?"

Well, I thought, *I'm a middle-aged widow with two kids and a husband who jumped off a bridge. I'm not really in a position to be choosy.* The idea of entering into a new relationship felt disloyal, treacherous. But part of me was intrigued. A man's amorous attention might be a fine distraction from my grief bubble and the slog of single parenting.

I soon received an email from Moungi Bawendi.

Hello Rachel,

Apparently, we have friends, or friends of friends, looking out for our social lives. These friends think that perhaps we might want to connect. It's not really something that I do... But this friend knows me pretty well and I trust her...I've started ice climbing this winter, and it occurred to me

*that meeting a stranger through friends can't be much more frightening
than being stuck on the ice 30 feet up not knowing what to do.*

He went on to say how deeply he was affected by Seth's death. Moungi
was born in Paris, grew up in the Midwest. His father was a Tunisian-
American mathematician. He got my attention.

I wrote back, trying to be fascinating and un-widowlike, not hiding
the fact of my extreme baggage, but also suggesting that I was vaguely
cool, or at least functional.

We agreed to meet at a café in Cambridge.

That's when I began to panic. I was so clearly unprepared. I hadn't
dated in 15 years. Were there new rules? Would I have to tell the kids?
What about an outfit? Contacts or glasses? What were his expectations?
What were mine? Why would he want to go out with me anyway? He
must be a loser.

I'd been advised by experts that my first foray back into romance
should be casual, low-stakes, with someone I wouldn't consider
relationship material. Moungi—with his Harvard degrees and fame in
the rarified world of nanotechnology—was too alluring. Clearly, I was
doing widowhood all wrong.

Only a few months after Seth's death, I had attempted casual
banter with strangers at a friend's wedding. I'd told myself it was time
to get back out there. Foolishly, I thought I'd made it past the roughest
patch, and the worst of it was over. Honestly, I was tired of wallowing.
A party, I imagined, might be just the ticket.

I'd chosen a strappy floral dress borrowed from a friend. But the
chill of fall had come early that year, and I found myself covered in
goosebumps and jealous of the other guests who'd wisely brought little
pastel throws and cotton scarves to wrap around their shoulders. I
tried talking to cleanly-scrubbed men in dark suits, but I never strayed
far from my own self-pity. The simple question, "What do you do?"

somehow led me back to death. "I'm a reporter," I'd say. "But I haven't been working on much lately, my husband died two months ago." This usually stopped any free-flowing conversation. Nonetheless, I felt an inexplicable need to tell every stranger about my plight. I might present as chatty and pulled together in my little heels and cute dress, but, in fact, my mind was six feet under.

It didn't take long to realize that celebrating at this moment was ridiculously out of reach. Drinking champagne felt good, then very bad. I projected my own dark reality onto the newlyweds. *This poor couple,* I thought, *so beautiful now, but without a clue. They likely believe, as I did, that their marriage will last and that over years, the systems and routines they build will offer stability. I bet they have faith that their vows will be binding, and, when children arrive, parenthood will be a protective glue. Ha. They're doomed.* I called a cab to take me home before the cake was served.

But for some reason, perhaps because of the endorsement from a trusted friend, or simply the passage of time, I was willing to try again.

My foreboding about the imminent date with Moungi escalated into dread as the date neared. I'd entered an unforgiving time machine where I was 15 again, a zaftig, insecure adolescent, frantically changing outfits, throwing each bad choice—the suggestive top, the all-black suit, the borrowed velvet—onto the bed and calling girlfriends to come over and help me. My brain was on fire, my body gripped by an adrenaline frenzy: *He won't like me, I'll never have sex again.* I tweezed like crazy, then complained to a friend who said I should be happy my nipple hair hadn't yet turned gray.

This is why people stay married, I thought, *why they stay in bad marriages, even, so they don't have to go through this turmoil.* My husband saw me give birth—twice—and shot video. After that, it didn't matter if I wore contacts or tweezed resolutely.

I settled on an outfit, and we met.

The moment I saw him, I thought, *He's too put together for me.* Moungi is tall, with a whiff of French grandeur and reserve, one of those guys who looks slim even in winter layers.

I barely clear five feet and carefully avoid bulky clothing. Though I considered leaving the café immediately, Moungi saw me, and smiled. What else could I do but smile back? We ordered—hot chocolate for him, tea for me. I prattled about my kids and my moods, feeling unkempt, hyper-conscious of my Brooklyn-Jewish-peasant roots, oversharing and bursting out of the little suit jacket I soon regretted choosing.

Moungi listened. He didn't seem rattled that most of my rambling kept leading back to death. Unable to edit myself, I shared my theory that Seth might have had bipolar disorder, explained that he was never diagnosed, but that there was a family history. I revealed my anxiety that this trauma would ravage my daughters' lives. Moungi took it all in. I didn't excuse myself to go feed the meter, afraid that his attentiveness, our connection, whatever was unfolding at our corner table—the promise of him, or someone like him, wise but brand new, alive and looking at me—would be lost. Three hours passed. I would get a parking ticket. But it seemed worth it.

Was this chemistry?

I guess the outfit was okay, and my rambling wasn't too scary, because we arranged a second date. A week later, we sat on barstools at the dimly-lit restaurant across town where Seth and I had celebrated my fiftieth birthday. Over prosecco and red lentil kibbeh, Moungi said he wanted to tell me something.

Years before, he'd been diagnosed with a type of blood cancer, but now, he explained, he was cancer-free: healthy, active, and with an excellent prognosis.

Later, on the phone, he said, "I hope I didn't freak you out too much."

Too late. I sank back into another sort of swivet. I can't date someone with cancer, I thought. I can't let death, or the threat of death, be part of a new relationship. I didn't want my person to die again. I wanted a guarantee. *Really, I deserved one*, I thought.

At night, alone in my bedroom, I chuckled aloud. Guarantee? Who gets that? My husband had been healthy and vibrant, loving and loved, and now he's dead. That guarantee unraveled like an old beach towel. *But, maybe*, I thought, *if the healthy guy died, might the cancer guy live?* That oddball logic seemed perfectly rational to me.

Still, I wanted some reassurance. In the past, my husband's mere presence had offered the sort of grounding I'd always craved. I needed someone to make me believe that everything would turn out fine.

One thing Moungi said kept returning to me: "Your kids could have been destroyed by this, but they seem to be doing all right." This kind remark offered reassurance of another sort. If he spoke it, maybe it was so.

Moungi's cancer was part of his story, like my husband's death was part of mine. We lived with it, and over years, its threat receded. And while I wouldn't say those facts were at all sexy, they do relate to sex in a way. The first time Moungi and I really kissed, in his kitchen, for nearly an hour, skin pressing against skin, with the kind of full-throttled desire that clears the debris of loss, it felt as if both of us were coming back to life, crawling out of some dark hole, blinking as we emerged from solitary confinement, clawing toward the light. We were two battered souls who'd seen death up close, with the kind of gut-clenching dread that compels you to grab your kids, steel yourself and hope that yours is not the one plane in a million going down.

Sex, I now see, is really the opposite of death. When it eventually happened with Moungi, I fell back into the sheets and laughed. It was shocking to feel so good. Was this allowed? Or was I, in some way, cheating on my husband?

Afterwards, I snuck back home, thinking this little affair would be my secret. It would be too confusing to tell the children about Moungi right now. I didn't want them to think their father could ever be, in any way, replaced. My narrative of loyalty—that Seth was my true and only love, even after death, would remain intact. This thing with Moungi was a side gig, a part-time arrangement, fully compartmentalized. *Still*, I thought, as I slipped under the covers and switched off the lights, *this pleasure could be a nice addiction*. I picked up my phone, stealthily, and texted: "Hey M., you in bed?" My heart quickened. I felt like a teenager—a confident younger me—awaiting his response.

Chapter 31

The White Coat

By the third year, our annual party for Seth had taken on a life of its own. I could rely on John's farro salad; Tal's homemade hummus, placed carefully on a hand-painted ceramic dish surrounded by fresh stalks of asparagus and sliced beets, whatever was fresh. Julia baked sweets and quiches. Everyone always showed up.

One element that shifted each year was the story I'd tell for the toast. This time, it was about a jacket.

We'd been on the Cape the previous Sunday, which would have been Seth's 53rd birthday. The girls had been huddled under a blanket on the living room couch, watching *High School Musical* for what felt like the millionth time. As Troy and Gabriella belted out yet another saccharine duet, my anxiety spiked. I'd been reading *The Times*—Trump, Russia, Hurricane Irma—unable to concentrate, and suddenly bolted upright and marched barefoot across the tile floor, feeling pin-pricks of sand lodge between my toes.

"We're taking a walk on the beach," I'd announced, snatching the blanket off their bodies. "Get up."

"No," they whined together.

"It's almost over," said Julia, "just let us finish."

"It's too cold," Sophia added, grabbing the ratty green, crocheted blanket up from the floor and pulling it around her neck. She was right. The wind had picked up, bringing with it a sharp chill. I didn't care. We had to get outside before two hours of immobilized movie-watching turned into an entire day.

"No, now," I said. Without fresh air, I thought I might keel over. "Let's go."

"Fine," said Julia, popping up. She marched over to the closet and grabbed an oversized coat. I heard the hanger drop to the ground. I spun around, looked at her, and gasped. The jacket she'd chosen was a white windbreaker with a blue striped lining that had been hanging in that closet over decades. Nothing special, except that it was the one Seth wore in a photograph taken a week before he died. Many of us in the family, his parents and brothers and a favorite aunt, now displayed this picture prominently in our homes because, in it, Seth looks like the happiest, most serene guy on the planet. His summer tan is accentuated by the coat's whiteness, and his dark chest hair is on full display with the coat zipped down to his sternum. Behind him, there's a grand sunset of pinks and oranges, wispy clouds turned deep purple over a midnight blue sea. It's impossible to believe the person in the picture is gone. This man framed by nature forms a portrait of vitality, even lustiness. So many life-affirming forces coming together: His eyes, the water, the waves he knew so well from childhood and through his own children. He radiates life. But the picture's power comes from what you know happens shortly after: darkness, despair, that fall.

I stared at Julia in the white coat, so big it dangled to her knees and hid her little body. My heart began to thrum rapidly, my rib cage felt near bursting. Part of my reaction was anticipating what might happen when Seth's parents, now in their 80s, stoic and clinging to routine as a means to cope with their youngest son's death, saw Julia in the jacket.

I began to shake my head vigorously. "Take off that coat, put on another one," I ordered. But Julia, slightly confused, planted her feet firmly on the ground.

"This one's cuddly—it's the warmest coat here, and there's a storm," she pointed toward the glass door, through which we could see the white-capped waves growing taller, more energetic. The wind had started rattling the house and we could hear the heavy wooden shutters clanking against the walls.

Despite Julia's reasonable argument, I believed wearing that coat was, simply, wrong. It belonged with Seth in the picture, not on a small girl.

We stood at an impasse for several minutes. I stared at Julia in the oversized jacket, then stared harder. I began to reconsider. A few years earlier, I would have raised my voice, barked at her:

Take. Off. That. Coat.

But in the three years that had passed, I realized, I'd been able to find more time to pause and think. *What if I stepped back, allowed Julia to reclaim the sad, tainted picture-coat?* She stared at me with her wide, chocolate eyes, and, in that momentary stand-off, a switch flipped. The old meaning I'd constructed around the coat began to lose its coherence, dissolving like a sand bar as the tide turned. A new possibility crystallized. I could make this decision right now, in this very moment. Perhaps this was no longer the jacket Seth wore on his final, peaceful day; maybe it was Julia's comforting windbreaker, the one she chose to wear on her father's birthday. Maybe it was both.

I stepped toward her, touching the droopy sleeve. "Okay," I said, "wear this one. It suits you."

At the end of the story, our guests nodded and dabbed their eyes. I looked over at my girls, who are never crazy about me telling tales in public about their private lives. But this time, I saw in their eyes a glimmer of approval. While they'd never admit it, I believe they understand why I do what I do, and how I constantly search for some meaning, even goodness, in our troubles.

Chapter 32

Dreaming of "Another Life"

Julia, like her father, is the youngest child. Also like him, when she latches on to an idea, she won't let go. Her teachers use words like "relentless" and "leader" and "fearless" to describe her. Her world is black and white, people are good or bad, stories end the right way or they are wrong.

Those traits were present in Julia when she was eight, and they remain. But so much else has changed. Her father will never know the particulars that shaped her, nor the small feats and accomplishments and yearnings that define her: how she became the baker of birthday cakes; her musical cameo as Jabba the Hutt; and how, by sheer will, she got herself a puppy.

* * *

On a brisk, sunny afternoon, Julia sat in the neighbors' yard, cradling their dachshund in her lap. She looked up at me longingly and I could see the start of a scheme forming. Like a prosecutor delivering the zinger that clinches the case, she stated bluntly: "We need another life in the house." Then she looked down at Piccolina, the dog. I shrugged my shoulders and offered a noncommittal but perky, "Maybe."

A few hours later, I observed Julia tucked into the corner of the couch investigating dog breeds online: maltipoos, goldendoodles, ginger spaniels, chocolate labs.

"So," she asked again, "how about that dog?" For days, all conversations lead back to this one. She stopped on the street to caress every neighborhood mutt we encountered, plopping her bum on the pavement and stuffing her face into each dog's neck.

This was Julia in third grade, her father only months dead. I would have done anything to make her happy. Still, I was fully aware of the downside of this particular wish of hers. I wrote a blog post about it: "Let's be clear," it began. "I need a dog like a hole in the head."

A dear aunt read the post and contacted me immediately. She said I was too fragile for a pet and reminded me—kindly but firmly—I was not a dog person. She offered alternatives: a fish, a cat. Had I considered a green-cheeked conure? She sent me a video of this parrot. I watched it with Julia. Her response: "When are we getting the dog?"

And who could blame her? You can't snuggle a parrot. She wanted the unconditional love she'd lost. I polled my friends; they leaned pro-dog.

"There is no rational reason to get a dog," said Sarah, who lived with a moody basset hound. "They are work, expense, and add to the list of beings in your home who have needs to be attended to. It is sort of like deciding to have a kid—no rational reason to do that either but big payoff on love, general hilarity, and a constant reminder of the joy in everyday small things." Another friend told me that dogs made her "more human." All that sounded great. And yet: someone's got to pick up their shit.

I hoped the record-breaking, 110-inches of snow that first winter might change Julia's mind about the dog. In the cold, we succumbed to chapped lips, dry faces. Static made our long hair defy gravity. As the snow days blurred together, I watched the clock through slow, aching hours. When we ventured out to play, we all knew who would have savored the storms more than anyone: their father, a sledding maven who never got cold and delighted the girls by drizzling maple syrup on freshly fallen snow served up in a big bowl for each of them.

Standing outside in wet boots watching them play, I imagined myself among the thick icicles hanging precariously from the eaves: frozen and dangerous. I turned into the kind of mother so burdened by circumstances that I couldn't discern the magic in their snow angels, or the beauty in their glistening faces, pink with cold. Searching for any sign of thawing, I was consumed with one bleak thought: Will this winter ever end?

Julia would peer out the window wistfully as Piccolina struggled to navigate the uneven landscape. But bad weather in no way mitigated her dog-yearning. "Now would be a great time," she said. "We could play in the snow together."

I began to cave under her pressure, and commenced a deeply-consuming search process. Soon, I had voicemail from dog breeders in Tennessee and North Carolina eager to arrange nonstop flights for the perfect bernedoodle puppy. A friend going through a divorce and needing a distraction became my personal dog matchmaker. She was gung-ho about finding us a pet, and annoyed when I hesitated. Then, at a dinner party, while I was kvetching about how truly ill-equipped I was to care for a puppy, an acquaintance mentioned she'd had a rabbit as a child. *They're cute, like dogs, but low maintenance*, she said.

The next day, my girls giddily perused the rabbits available for adoption on the House Rabbit Network website. They learned about a black-nosed, white "bachelor" called BooBoo, rescued from a "bad situation" who'd had his overgrown incisors removed. There was a bachelorette named Tokyo, an angora, who had "trust issues" and tended "to run and hide when humans entered the room." My kind of bunny.

We drove to a rabbit shelter in the suburbs, a dilapidated, unmarked shack, on a raw Saturday morning. Inside, a few kind, eager women, covered in fur, were volunteering their time. The dozens of rabbits appeared content, eating hay in their cages stacked one on top of another. It was dark and a bit depressing, but the smell wasn't as bad as I'd imagined. None of the rabbits were perfect, meaning they weren't the rabbits of fiction: cotton-tailed and fluffy, with delicate button noses. These were the rabbits that did not make the cut to star in some Easter Bunny film. They had super long ears, or massive snouts or fur so long it covered their faces. But we were on a mission to save a bunny, not judge a rabbit beauty contest.

Sophia was drawn to Marie, a grande dame, the size of a small dog, but with unnerving red eyes. Julia and I thought Marie was scary and that her eyes made her look like an alien. Also, Marie bit Julia's hand when she reached out to make friends. We moved on. Cherie was a mini-bunny, dappled brown, her physique like an oversized snail. Her ears were petite, her tail an iconic white tuft. Critically, she sat calmly in Julia's arms, and didn't seem to shed as much as the others. Her diet consisted of kale and greens, the volunteers explained, and she was housebroken. I said yes to Cherie—the French pedigree, real or imagined, clinched it—though my buyer's remorse kicked in as soon as I signed the adoption papers. Even as we ceremoniously renamed the rabbit Coco Zimmerman Teller, I told myself I could always return her, cruel as that might be.

Coco took her place in the family, roaming free around the house. Unfortunately, she did not effectively fill our void. As the first anniversary of Seth's death approached, Julia began to ask: "How did Daddy die?" I'd told the girls he'd died by suicide, but when I offered more details, Sophia consistently said she didn't want to hear about it, and shut down the conversation. Frankly, I was relieved. The details pained me, and I knew the story would hurt them, too.

I fretted over how to mark the first year. While worrying aloud to my friend Tal, she told me that she'd just rented a place in Provence for the summer; her husband would be teaching a philosophy course at the university nearby. "Come, stay with us," she said, her warmth so true and comforting. "We'd love it."

I said yes, which shocked the girls.

We spent those early summer days cooling off on massive alpine boulders fed by freshwater springs. In the evening, we'd gather outdoors for simple meals: salads with plump tomatoes, fresh olive oil and salt, warm baguettes and chilled local rosé.

On July 1, we woke up early to carry out the plan I'd concocted. We had spread out our fancy dresses the night before, so we could quietly slip away to the Marc Chagall museum in Nice. His paintings reverberated with color as if in motion; even the children were drawn in. They snapped photos of the deep blue *Creation of Man*, the glowing red of *Paradise*. Afterwards, we snuck outside to the back of the building. Security guards surrounded the place, but somehow, we found a hidden spot. Together, we created a circle of stones and stuck a candle in the ground. I lit a match, mindful of escape routes should one of the guards catch us in the act.

As the candle burned we talked about Seth: the performances he'd missed, the achievements of the year. Then, one by one, we leaned over and told him we'd love him forever, and, in unison, blew out the flame.

As we packed up to fly home, Julia once again raised the question. "How did Daddy die?"

"Please, not here," Sophia begged.

I told them to keep packing, this wasn't the right time.

On the plane, Julia pressed me.

"Now can you tell me how he died?"

"Really, on the flight?" Sophia rolled her eyes.

I promised Julia I'd tell her when we got home. She took me literally: the night after we'd arrived back in Cambridge, just before bedtime, she walked into my bathroom. "Mommy, how did he die?"

I couldn't duck or delay any longer. I took a deep breath and got down on my knees, so we'd be eye to eye. "Well, baby...his body fell from a very high place, and his heart stopped before he hit the ground, so he didn't feel it. He jumped," I said, "off a bridge." She looked at me, her big eyes—his eyes—began to tear up. I held her, and the hurt grew. But after a few moments, she disentangled herself from my arms.

"You know the first thing I thought when you said that?" she said.

"What, honey?"

"I thought of Daddy leaf jumping."

Then I began to cry. Each fall, Seth would gather huge armfuls of dried leaves and create an impressive mound. He'd lead the girls outside and the three of them would take turns jumping. There were many variations: a flip jump, a twist, a cannonball into the leaves. They did this at the park across the street, or at Seth's childhood home in Connecticut, or near his office on campus.

"Yes, sweetheart, I thought of leaf jumping too," I said. Then, trying to add a positive spin: "And you know another thing I thought of? Remember how Dad always wanted to fly? I'm not sure, but I imagine, for a moment, or at least a few seconds, he actually felt like he was flying."

Julia nodded.

We crawled into my bed, and I wrapped my body around her.

"Are you sad that I told you?"

"No, I wanted to know. Can I ask another question? If he parked on the bridge, why didn't anyone try to stop him?"

"That's a great question, darling. I just don't know."

I let the news settle. Then I called Sophia into the room.

"Now Julia knows exactly how Dad died," I said, "and maybe you already know, too. Either way, I want you to promise to talk with her if she ever wants to talk about it. Because you are sisters. Because this is something you can help each other with."

"Yes," Sophia said, understanding the magnitude of my request. "I will do that."

Both girls absorbed Seth's death in such different ways, I realized. This meant I had to be vigilant about who needed what. It was Julia, most often, who demanded facts and details. She was the one who trudged faithfully with me for two years to that support group for grieving families. For both of us, the group offered perspective. Julia told me it was good to know she wasn't alone. I found that sitting in a circle of pain made me feel better, too, in a twisted, human way. It showed me that other people suffered just like me, and that, in fact, there could be a hierarchy of suffering. In my group, one woman's husband was beaten to death. Another husband was found in a frozen river. A shy woman, who often trembled, spoke of keeping her dead husband's laundry in a basket near her bed—for five years—even after she'd moved to a different house. In another family, the daughter was the first to find her father's body after his suicide.

I learned that things could be worse in the circumstances of death, but also in the reality of the lives left behind. Maybe Julia saw this too, in a child's way. I knew there were tangible factors that altered our trajectory and massively buffered our distress, and most of them boiled down to money.

We were able to remain in the East Cambridge house the kids grew up in, leaning on its safe familiarity. Seth's life insurance, with its generous payout, allowed me to continue with my part-time job, and not worry about cash flow for some time. The children could remain at the private school they'd started as 4-year-olds, again bolstering us with continuity and community. At the end of third grade, I hugged Julia's teacher, who had watched over her, kept her safe, and often called me with updates and sightings—*Julia's on the monkey bars, Julia's giggling with a friend.* "Thank you for saving Julia," I said. She replied, "Julia saved herself."

Other single mothers in the grief group did not have these resources. Their kids attended schools where teachers were overwhelmed by the size of their classes and couldn't take special care of the silent, withdrawn child in the back row. Mothers were forced to move into smaller, more confined spaces, further from friends or family support. Some weren't allowed time off from work to take their distraught children to counselors or trauma specialists. Others couldn't afford any outside interventions at all. Money didn't solve our problems, but it certainly softened their impact.

I also saw that in death, gender matters. At least in my group, the widowed men seemed far more forlorn. In some cases, they'd been left to parent as if for the first time. "I've never made a sandwich for my kid," one dad said. "I don't have the words for a depressed teenage girl," said another.

For us, on a superficial level, nothing changed. If you peered through a window at our lives, before and after, you'd see a similar scene: a harried woman packing lunches each morning, driving the kids to school, on the phone scheduling doctor's appointments and playdates, peering at a laptop, awaiting inspiration. The only difference, if you looked closely, is that you wouldn't spot the father.

***

Social scientists talk about "gain spirals," the idea that one lucky break can beget more of the same, and in this accrual of upward momentum, a patina of protection and resolve forms. Our tangible financial and social supports created such gain spirals, and I clung to them fiercely.

And so, even after death, our lives continued. The girls were small, agile, jaunty when they lost their father; they could easily scramble to the top of his shoulders, using him as a diving board into the ocean. Then, before my eyes, they had curves, breasts, and deodorant in their travel bags.

Julia started thinking about her professional future, what she might become. A classmate suggested she should be mayor, because she was concerned about everyone and demanded justice for all. She aimed higher. Not mayor, she said: "President."

That career goal might have been somewhat unrealistic, given that her knowledge of history was, in large part, based on television. I'd allowed many hours of movies and shows as a way for her to disengage from the world. But I saw the result of this when Sophia, preparing for an exam, quizzed her sister on important moments in U.S. history: "What illness was not well known in the '80s but later swept through the country and the world?"

"AIDS," said Julia. "I know that from Richard and Ellis's flashbacks on *Grey's Anatomy.*"

Or, "What was an unpopular war in the late '60s?"

Julia said: "Duh, the Vietnam War—they talked about it on *That '70s Show.*"

She also embraced dark humor as a way to cope. When, late at night, her entire foot swelled from what was likely a wasp bite and I started prepping for a trip to the ER, Julia shook her head at me. "I'm *fine*," she said, her elevated foot resembling a large Italian sausage.

"How do you know you're fine?" I said. More head shaking from Julia. I started Googling heel tumors, cellulitis, rare poisonous insects of Eastern Massachusetts. I sent close ups of her ballooning foot to my doctor friend. "Actually," Julia said, "I'm fine and you're not. I looked it up on CrazyMoms.com and it said so right there."

A few years later, when schools shut down and the world went topsy-turvy, Julia's mood sank as the losses mounted: the canceled play she starred in; the denial of a true goodbye to school friends; days without physical release; sickness and death all around. I felt the reverberations of Seth and wondered how far Julia might descend. I heard her tiny voice from the past: "We need another life in the house."

Yes, we did. So, finally Julia prevailed, and after years of waiting, she got her puppy. Phoebe the labradoodle is a diva, devoted, insanely soft, and, with her milky-white curls and pale apricot ears, reminiscent of a Creamsicle.

Phoebe was also more work than I ever imagined. She hated her crate and whimpered to be set free at 4am. Chewed-up rug bits littered the house; in the air, there was a vague, noxious scent from whatever she'd rolled in outside. After a few months, the vet prescribed Gabapentin for the dog's anxiety, 200 milligrams a day. Phoebe began sleeping in my bed, and sometimes, in the middle of the night, would throw up an indigestible fragment of garbage, like a plastic Slim Jim wrapper or a velvet hair scrunchie. But when Julia pressed her face into the puppy's warm belly and kissed her wet mouth, I saw Phoebe as a long-lost doll, pure and captivating, like girlhood itself, restored to its rightful place.

Chapter 33

What You've Missed

Her first period
My last period (it wasn't so bad)
A solo ukulele performance that brought grownups to tears
Crop tops
Arguments over crop tops
The shock of your child telling you something you don't already know
THC-infused chocolates in the basement (a friend's, she says)
A lead in the high school musical

* * *

You've missed 15. Let me tell you what it's like.

Sophia's dabbing her cheekbones with a cleansing cloth in a kind of reverie, carefully examining the state of her pores in my bathroom mirror as she readies herself for sleep.

She just washed her hair, which hangs in thick, wet plaits past her shoulders, jet black—just like yours. A loose *Charlotte's Web* T-shirt hangs off one shoulder, creamy and unblemished like bone china. I walk in, startled: my daughter isn't normally in my bathroom at night. She doesn't look up as I enter, hardly even moves, unwilling to disturb the inexorable magnetism between the mirror and her face.

You last saw her at 11, a fifth grader, dressed in baggy nylon sports shorts and oversized men's jerseys that hid her figure. She played touch football at recess with the boys and was surprisingly good, gaining respect for her speed and strategies on the field. When the ball got lost in the trees, the games ceased and she grew glum. Then you delivered a new football to the classroom: a hero.

I approach her cautiously, not knowing which aspect of my adolescent daughter I will encounter. "Oh, you're here," I say, and she continues her ablutions undeterred. I'm pleased that she allows me the rare treat of watching her attend to her own body. More often, she snaps back into a defensive stance when I arrive, or marches off, shutting me out swiftly, like a sudden blackout in a lightning storm.

She glances over, and with the grace that accompanies the settling of one's body into its adult form, she steps toward me. I notice her bare feet, tiny, the same size six as mine, and make a mental note to ask about my new suede boots that have recently gone missing.

She tucks her hair behind one ear in a way that recalls her younger self; shy, awkward, and less aware of her effect on others.

"Mom," she says, "I need to ask you something."

I focus on my daughters' lustrous hair, already rich and full at birth, which triggers in me a warm thrill at her familiarity.

"Sure," I say, "What is it?"

She moves so close I can smell her breath, sweet with spearmint.

"I don't know how to say this, so I'm just going to say it," she says.

I steady myself, expecting—Jesus—who knows what?

"I think I should get an IUD."

"Okay. Wow. Honey, sure, can we talk about it?"

"You're not mad?"

"I'm not mad."

She picks up the brush, re-adjusts her hair and reconnects with the mirror, satisfied. "Just so you know, I'm not having sex, and I'm not going to for a while."

"I'm glad to hear that," I say, exhaling audibly. "So why do you need an IUD?"

"The doctor says it's a good idea." (Another mental note: call, or rather yell, at this doctor for failing to warn me of a major, sex-related decision during what had been the first appointment my daughter ever had without me present.)

"Oh, so let's keep talking about it."

"Thanks for not being one of those crazy moms who starts screaming and yelling and immediately says 'No.'"

If she knew about my early sex life—with a random guy I met on a train in France, for instance, oblivious to consent, unprotected and fully fueled by pot and rebellion—she would better understand my cool reaction.

As her father, your response would be different. I believe you dreaded the complexity of teenage daughters. I wonder, now, how you'd have handled your 15-year-old's request for birth control. You'd want to meet the guy, if there was one, inspect him in a 1950s dad manner, ask about intentions, or perhaps, convince your daughter to wait a little longer. I wonder what heroics you'd stage to try to alter her decision.

It's the small details of our reality you've missed, like at 7am, when I've been up for an hour preparing lunches: almond and peanut butter sandwiches with bananas and honey, cucumber tomato salad, a maple snack bar for one, a blueberry yogurt for the other. As I start slicing oranges for breakfast, Sophia saunters in, texting, not looking up, wearing robin's egg blue shorts and a low-cut, lacy white tank top completely inappropriate for biking through Cambridge. I take a deep breath. Mostly, I've given up telling her what to wear.

I've asked her to activate the location tracker on her phone. I love the idea of knowing exactly where my daughter is at every moment of the day. As an engineer, you might have liked this too, but more for the clever technology and less for the lurking. I don't care about its

Orwellian trappings, though. Her late arrivals and unanswered calls make my heart stop and give me bouts of diarrhea.

The truth is, your death merely heightened my long run with anxiety. Before, I worried about things I thought I could control; now I worry more, knowing I have no control at all.

When we fell in love, I was at the height of my bravery, a reporter crusading around the world seeking "truth." In the '90s and early 2000s, I flew on sketchy national airlines to report stories in Africa and China, to Cuba on a Russian plane shored up with duct tape. After 9/11, when I walked to work across the Brooklyn Bridge and watched as the second plane plowed into the World Trade Center, air travel completely lost its glamour. But it was only after the children were born that I developed a full-blown, debilitating fear of flying. I cancelled vacations and pretended to be sick to avoid it. I forced the kids to take the train from Orlando to Boston—round trip—trying to make it seem like a grand adventure.

You indulged my fears, grudgingly, allowing last minute flight changes and ditched plans. But it also made you tense with frustration. How many times did you implore me to focus on statistics? "It's safer than driving," you'd say, "just be rational," as if I could easily turn that kind of dispassionate thinking on and off. These became familiar stock characters for us to inhabit: the clear-thinking, logical husband paired with the wildly emotional, irrational wife.

Still, there were times when we agreed about the risks of daily life. I always appreciated your stern warnings that the children should be more careful crossing the street, biking around the neighborhood, swimming in strong riptides.

This is something I miss about our marriage: the shared worrying— not the worrying part, but the mutuality of bonding through heightened fears, the co-mingling of anxieties because *our* children were at stake. We each had a distinct relationship with risk, but we shared reassurances, acknowledged each other's fears, and never, fully, left the other to worry alone.

I'm thinking of a time when Sophia, just 10, was invited to a friend's house in the woods of Western Massachusetts. Do you remember? It was her first long weekend away and we'd agreed she'd phone us that evening to say goodnight. We grew concerned when she didn't call. We rang the friend's house, called both parents' cell phones and texted again and again. It got late, 11pm, midnight. Maybe they went to a movie, we thought, lying in bed. Our tension rose, and we grasped for explanations. Thinking the phones went out, we called the local telephone company, but there were no outages reported.

By 1am we'd reached a frenzied state. "I'm checking the local accident reports online," I said, as you exiled yourself in the office for distraction. Finally, about an hour later, I blurted out a suggestion. "I know this sounds crazy, but what if I just call the state police?" I braced myself for your response, expecting the usual taunt that I was being irrational.

Instead, you surprised me. "Okay, do it."

Energized, we succumbed to our disaster scenarios and phoned the cops. "Hi," I said, as chirpy as possible. "This is probably nothing, but we can't reach our daughter and no one answers at the house and we're concerned." It must have been a slow night at the Northampton Police Barracks, because the dispatcher agreed to send a guy over to check things out. A trooper showed up at the family's house and knocked on the door. Soon after, we got an email from the kid's father: "Hi, just got awakened by a state trooper. Everyone is asleep, but our landline is out and we don't get cell reception here. What's going on??"

Yes, we felt stupid and embarrassed, and no, that friendship didn't last. But at least we knew our daughter was safe.

The day after the family returned from the woods and dropped Sophia back home, a bomb exploded at the finish line of the Boston Marathon. As reports of destruction and death rolled across our screens, and the entire city was ordered to lock down while a manhunt raged in our neighborhoods, I learned something that I think about often. It's generally not the things you fear that hurt you—a child lost in the woods, an errant flight—it's the things you can't even imagine that rise up, suddenly, to haunt you.

Now, I am left to worry alone, with no reinforcements. I've lost the naïve acceptance that an off-handed, bedtime, "See you in the morning," can ever be fully trusted.

I get walloped by persistent night terrors that, despite my vigilance, I've missed the thing that could have offered protection. When my child is 10 minutes late, my brain rushes immediately to the worst: kidnapped, knocked out, bleeding.

During our marriage, I worried that our differences might undo us—contrasting parenting styles, opposite sleep schedules, disagreements over food. Never once did I worry about you jumping off a bridge. Then, that morning, I left you reading *The Times* on the couch, and now you're gone. This shocks me still.

My fear landscapes seem silly to my 15-year-old daughter. For her, risk is a distant abstraction. She doesn't call me to check in as she bikes through the streets of downtown Boston. She doesn't respond when she's late and I phone her over and over again. After 20 calls that go to voicemail, I set out to search for her, envisioning catastrophe: her limp body along Storrow Drive, her bicycle, mangled. When I finally reach her (phone dead, ringer off) I can practically hear her rolling her eyes at my overwrought behavior. "I'm okay, Mom," she says, "it's okay."

Would you have gone after her, too?

She halfheartedly agrees to the location tracker, though she finds the whole idea offensive. She's promised to turn it on, but in the morning, while we're both rushing around, she snaps: "I'm late, let's deal with it tonight."

I struggle to enable the proper notifications, but haven't a clue, and she's out the door saying she'll leave without the phone and I'm following her saying, "No, you won't. You're doing this *my* way!"

She says: "Listen to yourself, you sound insane."

I say, "I don't like your tone," then physically thrust my body in her path so she can't escape, but she does and now she grabs the phone and I grab it back and we are screaming with a bicycle between us and she's staring at me like she wants to wring my neck and I try to pull the bike away from her and it ricochets back and bangs her thigh and she says I hurt her and I'll be sorry. I make her apologize and she does but doesn't mean it and bikes off in a fury.

Later she texts me: "What you did this morning was cruel and disgusting. You hurt me and I cried all the way to the bus. I hope you're happy." Then she informs me that she is considering calling the crisis hotline to report my "domestic abuse." I'm not quite sure what happened between me cutting up the orange slices and now being reported to the authorities. I play out the possibilities. None look good.

You would have hated my behavior, and hers. You'd try to impose rules and punishments, and, unlike me, you'd probably follow through. I am a failed disciplinarian. I take away her phone, and immediately regret it: not only do I lose contact, but so does she, with the friends that constitute her safety net and help her muddle through these tough years, the girls who FaceTime her when she doesn't get the part she'd dreamed of, or when the cool guy's attention fades.

In the end, she doesn't call the abuse hotline, and we survive this fight, and the ones that follow.

We come apart and back together, my teenage daughter and me. We scream, and then we watch *Sleepless in Seattle* huddled under blankets, our sweet tea and jam-filled cookies balancing on our knees. Once, we run along the beach side-by-side. I say something stupid and she jogs ahead of me, so thoroughly frustrated by her senseless mother. I continue running, further than we would have run together, and it takes some time for me to return to our usual finish line. When I finally get there, she is waiting for me, on the road, searching for my figure to appear. She walks toward me: "I thought you were run over by a car or something," she says.

I respond: "Welcome to my world."

She asks a family friend to take her for driving lessons in Cambridge. This friend comes to me, self-consciously, and says that the best place for this is Mount Auburn Cemetery. There, she can practice turns and stops with no traffic and few pedestrians. Of course, it's also where you're buried, next to a great, old beech tree. I ask my daughter if she feels okay driving there. She shrugs: "It's just a place."

Then, she's performing on stage, and for a moment, we lock eyes. She commands the room with her voice, her beauty. I kvell. I can't help it. I lean over to the stranger next to me and tell her that's my daughter singing. She congratulates me.

And here's the thing I miss most of all: the overflow of pride I cannot share with you, her father, the reality that no one else in the world loves her like we do, the cold truth that she's lost your unwavering gaze.

Chapter 34

Chemistry

When I started seeing Moungi, we kept our relationship secret. Each encounter in those early days felt illicit: a viewing of the Rothkos in Harvard Square was more about a quick brush of his body against mine; a dance concert in Boston became memorable when we simultaneously grabbed each other's hands rushing to catch the T. When we kissed late at night, leaning against his car, I looked around instinctively, to see who might be watching. To the extent it made my limbs go weak, this affair couldn't possibly be allowed. Maybe not a high crime, but surely a misdemeanor.

I believed I'd masterfully taken on the cloak of widowhood, had excelled in the role of the single mom. I could do this, I thought, for the rest of my life. There's a certain standing one gains as a woman on her own: a tough, don't-fuck-with-me cover. Playing the widow card was a pretty sure bet when berating Bank of America for overcharges, or justifying my rude behavior to front desk staff when the doctor ran late, or when I decided to cancel last minute on friends. But if I was a put-upon widow, how could I also inhabit such mouth-watering personal pleasure?

Beyond that, I wasn't convinced that the girls would be keen on their mom having a boyfriend. We'd placed pictures of Seth in all corners of the house, we talked about him freely, lovingly, remembered his foibles and fierce devotion, what made him laugh. Where would another man fit in?

208 – RACHEL ZIMMERMAN

But Moungi was in no rush. I noted his patience and steadiness. He listened closely. Even if I screamed and curled up in a chair asking a string of *whys*, Moungi remained rooted.

He didn't appear flustered when I'd tell him about my overreactions to the kids' petty fights over clothing or who got the shower first. Once, when Sophia accidentally spilled a full bag of flour all over the floor, I snapped and threw a towel at her. She reminded me of this periodically, as evidence of my bad parenting.

Moungi's mere existence seemed to absorb this excess volatility. It was like I'd been laying on a bed of nails, then suddenly someone slipped a thick luxurious mattress under my body. I began to sleep less fitfully, with fewer internal alarm bells startling me awake at 3am.

When I finally told the children I was seeing a guy, they were blasé. They wanted pictures and details about his daughter. As long as I was there to tuck them in at night and zip them around town and cheer the loudest at every performance, my dating, in theory, was no problem. And, they likely figured, with Moungi around, someone else might take care of me.

After we'd been dating about six months, Moungi and I decided our children should meet. We arranged a low-pressure group outing: *Pitch Perfect 2*, the movie. A capella at the local multiplex, what could go wrong? The film opens with "Fat Amy" high up on a ladder performing in a sing-off, her butt at the center of the frame. When Amy's leggings suddenly split wide open, exposing her underwear, my hands turned clammy. I sat in my reclining seat next to Moungi, behind the girls, straining my neck trying to discern their reaction. This movie choice, I suddenly thought, confirmed my substandard parenting. I was admittedly lax in what I allowed the kids to watch—"chazerai," my mother would call it, essentially schlock. I was certain the crassness of *Pitch Perfect 2* would tank our carefully crafted girl-bonding plan, but the kids didn't seem bothered by the bad taste. They loved the movie. We emerged from the theater into the sun and the three girls each gave the film a thumbs up.

Then, we climbed into our separate cars and drove home. When Moungi and I talked on the phone later, we considered it a success.

As our relationship grew stronger, it was my kids he worried about. "What if they get attached and I get sick again?" At this point, he'd not crossed the five-year post-cancer mark. He didn't want to be the one to deliver another devastating loss to the girls. I considered this and agreed that another death would be intolerable. But we made out on his couch anyway. Because lust is not reasonable.

When a friend clumsily asked me what the difference was between Seth and Moungi, I said: "Moungi is alive." It was kind of a joke, but not really. There was no comparison; it wasn't an either/or. Yet, in the way humans do, I tried to match them up, side by side. Seth was an engineer who threw himself at problems again and again, sometimes brutally, until they were fixed. Moungi's work was more silent and subtle, about shining a powerful light on cancerous tissue, for instance, to gain a granular clarity, a more faithful picture. When he looked at me and told me I was beautiful, I felt seen, because seeing is what Moungi does.

Unlike me, he is lean and chiseled, with the lithe dancer's stature I always wanted. If we had kids together, they might have been taller. But the fact that we don't have kids together is liberating. We eluded the sleep-deprived phase, the no-sex-because-it's-become-too-predictable era, and the ongoing, small disagreements that erode romance over decades. We experienced each other not in the genetics of our children, but in the here and now. He's sterile, I'm well past menopause: we're a perfect match! Of course, with teenage girls, it's never a picnic, but our roles were so exquisitely delineated: you raise your kid, I'll raise mine. And in the meantime, I'll back you up.

We fell deeply in love.

Our first Christmas together, we'd planned a grand vacation to Hawaii. Moungi had miles, the flights would be free; it all seemed to fall into place. We would meet on Kauai, where we'd hike along the

Napali coast and surf with the girls in Poipu. He flew out first, with his daughter. "See you soon!!" he texted.

But a few days before the trip, Julia started coughing and vomiting, then I got sick too. The idea of a long flight with a sick child seeped into my psyche. I frantically called the airline to reschedule and phoned doctors hoping they'd forbid my travel, get me off the hook.

If I'd been a different kind of parent, I'd have offered Julia a big gulp of Benadryl, swallowed some myself, and boarded the plane. But my fear of flying suffused with the specter of illness overwhelmed my feverish brain. The unknowns of this trip and this relationship—my lack of control—grated on me until I couldn't tell if I was really sick or just making myself sick with worry. It didn't much matter. I called Moungi and spit out my saga. He listened quietly. I prepared for a backlash, but he was lovely, said he understood, told me there'd be other trips to beautiful, lush bays. "Just get better," he said, "take care of yourself."

The following year, we aimed lower and flew three hours to Florida. On the beach, we snapped a picture of the five of us in swimsuits as a holiday card. It was the first shot of us all together, and somehow, the picture made us true. The kids practiced back tucks on the sand and Moungi and I sat in our chairs holding hands under a towel. We had sex every night, though we had separate bedrooms because Julia still preferred it that way. He'd slip in late, once the children were asleep. "We should sleep, too," he'd say, but then we were kissing, in that dozy way, my hair a wild array of sun-streaked waves on the pillowcase. We dissolved into each other, so close we couldn't tell whose limbs were whose. Why sleep now, why stop?

When, having dated a few years, we moved into his house, it was initially under the pretense of a flood in my kitchen that required months of heavy remediation. It was either Moungi's or the Days Inn. The choice was clear. But I slept in my own room and snuck into his bedroom only after checking that the coast was clear. Things were going well until it appeared that his daughter was allergic to our rabbit. We relocated the rabbit to a friends' house, and, just when my kids' resentment began to rise, discovered her allergy was a false alarm. Coco returned, triumphant.

I still hedged a bit when we finally moved into his house legitimately. We'd packed enough to get by—a few boxes of books and clothes and treasured possessions—but left most of our stuff behind. Maria moved in to our old house, which allowed me to avoid the psychic toll of saying goodbye to our Seth-home, and also provided a Plan B. If things with Moungi didn't work out, we could always move back.

Shockingly, we adjusted with relative ease. Each girl got her own bedroom and a drawer in the bathroom. Moungi helped my kids with their math homework and tried to teach them basic bicycle maintenance. Under his watch, they mastered the art of crepe-making, zesting limes for a blueberry ricotta filling that left them with blue tongues, begging for more.

For the first time in my life, I lived in a house with a garden. The parsley and basil delighted me, the patio tomatoes were a late summer orgy. The peonies, pale pink and magenta and white with yellow centers, formed an outrageous tableau as they suffused the walkway with their commanding perfume. The garden was so exotic to me that I was compelled to call my father; the notion of us, two Brooklynites discussing flowers, made us both laugh with the absurdity of how far I'd traveled.

The garden was one thing, but, of course, full-fledged family blending required actual time and effort. It was all adjustments and compromises. I finally moved into Moungi's bedroom officially, and we tried to work out five irreconcilable schedules. We negotiated amongst the vegetarians, vegans, and carnivores, the late sleepers and early risers, the slobs and neat freaks, and intervened in the inevitable flare-ups of three girls sharing a bathroom. I hummed Sister Sledge's, "We Are Family," shimmying my body to the words.

Sometimes, a wave of sadness knocked me off balance. When I heard the chords of a certain Adele song on the car radio; when Moungi picked up a frisbee and threw it to one of my girls; every time his daughter called him "Daddy," I thought about Seth, now a father-memory, that other, fainter man on the beach long ago. His phantom presence began to take its place in the family. *Maybe,* I thought, *we could live with that, too.*

Chapter 35

Whatever Makes You Feel Good

It happened slowly, but after a few years back at work, I noticed I'd been avoiding my boss, taking the long way around to the bathroom so I wouldn't pass his office. At some point, it dawned on me that pretty much every time he assigned me a story I felt sick. I no longer had any interest in scoops or snippets of news. "Is this really a story?" I'd ask when he told me to pull together a short piece on, say, a new hospital wing, or the hot local biotech's quarterly earnings. I craved depth and import: how poor kids with cancer have worse health outcomes, the insidious way ZIP codes can determine access to the best treatment, why home health aides are paid so atrociously. I started oversharing with sources, talking about Seth's suicide over tea at their kitchen tables, thinking, as I spoke, of the many professional norms I was violating. One woman gave me a CD of her daughter, a singer and composer; I showed her video of Sophia on stage. My supervisor wanted me to produce more—faster—but I was unable to ramp up production like I could years before.

Sometimes I'd think that Seth's death was the sole reason behind my shifting perspective on the news and my role as a reporter. It certainly was one factor: Life, it became clear, was short, and I'd lost patience for the trivial. But simply getting older also changed me. My appetite for breaking news, for writing "objectively" about tiny slices of the world, had waned. Sometimes this felt like failing. But it also allowed a certain freedom. A writer friend whose child had died very young offered her view: If you can survive tragedy, she said, you earn a kind of free pass.

Her advice: "Do whatever makes you feel good."

I quit the radio station and took a job writing for a woman I'd long admired, a visionary MacArthur "genius" who advocated for a broader definition of "health care" that included nutritious food, safe housing, a reliable job. When that gig ended, I started writing for another non-profit, one whose guiding principle is that all people deserve the kind of care that the privileged among us can readily access.

Part of me felt diminished, with my reporter's ambition and competitive drive shriveled. I continued to freelance on the side, not wanting to give up journalism completely, but that felt insignificant. I could no longer check the journalist box in good faith. Still, it was refreshing to express my beliefs out loud, advocate for what was right. The girls were constant cheerleaders: "You're still writing, Mom, so it counts."

Chapter 36

Our Stories

As we lingered in the parked car before rehearsal, Sophia described her part in the upcoming play, *This, I Know For Sure*. The content, developed by theater students at her high school, was personal and intense: rape, social isolation, violence. "Bring tissues," she told me. Her section was about Seth, memory, and loss. I asked if she needed help, or if there were any gaps I could fill in. She said: "Are you asking if I have questions about my story? No. It's my story."

The title of her vignette was "My Sunshine," and, in it, she evoked a scene of herself as a small child on a sunny family vacation, sitting at the edge of a pool, throwing a beach ball back and forth with her dad. She was warm and content playing this simple game—until Seth threw the ball a little too far. When she leaned over to catch it, she fell in the pool. She couldn't swim at the time, and struggled to breathe. "I feel like I'm drowning," she said in the play. Seth jumped in to save her. Then her focus shifted, and she began singing "You Are My Sunshine" as if she was being rocked to sleep.

A Greek chorus of boys, representing Seth, appeared behind her. "Remember what you used to say?" she asked them, and the chorus replied: "I can fix anything but a broken heart." She began the song again, but with different lyrics: "You are my sunshine, my only sunshine. And I miss you every day. You said you could fix anything but a broken heart…You weren't there to fix mine."

Julia and I sat smack in the middle of the theatre on opening night, just a few rows back from the stage. She rested her head on my shoulder during her sister's piece, and we cried together because we remembered so clearly his promise to fix what was broken; because high school boys were saying his words, not him; because we believed he would be there, always—and now knew he'd never be there again.

It was revelatory to me when my daughters began telling stories that were their own, narratives that were separate, and sometimes at odds, with mine. These stories had become their property, like a row of hillside cottages for which I had no key. I still tried to exert control, convinced that I remained the expert on storytelling, but I saw them begin to claim the territory of their memories, relying on their own words and interpretations.

This realization reminded me of a research study I'd written about years earlier, on the tangible benefits of storytelling. This work suggested that people's mental health improved when they "took control" of their own stories; when they intentionally reframed their thinking in ways that put them in the driver's seat of their lives rather than at the mercy of the capricious whims and hardships of existence. Essentially, it's not the particular story that matters, but rather, how we tell it to ourselves.

I'd mulled over this theory often since Seth's death, because it hinted at the alluring possibility that we might actually have some control over our lives. The study's author, Jonathan Adler, a psychologist at the Olin College of Engineering just outside Boston, had become one of my go-to sources. He'd explained to me how each of us is, of course, the main character in our own stories, but also, the narrator—and critically, a narrator with options. This made it possible to revise one's own story with certain narrative elements that could make us healthier: a sense of agency and purpose, the ability to integrate illness and loss into our identity and still get out of bed in the morning. Adler found that the specific ups and downs each of us face have less of an impact on our health than the words we use to describe these events.

The striking part, he'd said, is that as the people in his study began recasting their stories with more agency, they reported improvements in their mood. It was as if they told a new story and then "lived their way into it." This was not simply a matter of Pollyanna-ish positivity when things looked bleak, not just an attitude adjustment that turned a "bad" story into a "good" one. Instead, it was about identifying what was life-affirming while also acknowledging the vexing twists of grief and pain we all experience.

I think about this work again, when it dawns on me that I now have a different answer to Sophia's question from all those years ago: "Will we ever be happy again?" I wake up some mornings and the answer is *yes*. Seth's death remains in us but no longer defines us.

I recently rediscovered a hardcover book given to me as a child. *Jane's Blanket*, written by the playwright Arthur Miller for his daughter, is the story of a soft, tattered baby blanket Jane adored and refused to throw away even as she grew older. After many years, her parents tossed the ragged blanket in the trash, only to find that a family of birds had retrieved it, repurposed the cloth shreds to build a nest in a tree outside Jane's window. A similar sense of renewal took root in me as Seth appeared in new forms. He had become a cherished remnant, the vestige of a past love, even as his centrality continued to diminish. Over time, the facts and hard details of his "case" have receded in my mind, while the contours of our newfangled lives began to take shape. My kids and I remained a tight power trio, a singing, dancing girl-group, but somehow, we'd landed on a new, ever-shifting stage, finding our footing, holding our balance.

* * *

I was wholly unprepared for the news about Sophia's next theatre endeavor. On an early spring afternoon, she called, out of breath, to tell me she'd been offered the role of Martha "Dumptruck" Dunnstock in *Heathers*, the dark '80s satire about fatally toxic high school alliances. For a full minute, I couldn't speak. I thought: *What are the odds that my daughter gets cast as a bullied high school girl who attempts suicide by jumping off a bridge?*

"That's great, honey," I said flatly, having no other choice, I felt, but to support her creative pursuits.

"Why don't you sound more enthusiastic," she snapped back.

Well, duh, as one of the Heathers might say.

Here's what I didn't say: This scenario is one of my recurring nightmares—that my daughter, traumatized by her father's death, would become the bullied high school girl, hobbled by insecurity, self-doubt, torment.

At night, after rehearsals, I'd ask how she was doing, emotionally. She would not indulge me with this discussion. "I just want to make sure you're okay," I said. "The material is a little close to home." Eyeroll. Then: "Mom, I'm an actor. This is a character. It's not me."

In the musical, Martha clung to one sweet memory from kindergarten: The boy she liked presented her with a scab off his scraped knee and she carefully placed it in a locket that hung near her heart. Martha's big solo, "Kindergarten Boyfriend" concluded that "certain girls are meant to be alone." She sang about obliterating her sorrow in a nap that's "centuries long."

As the final "oohs" of the song trailed off, my daughter-as-Martha stood high above the audience on the edge of a raised platform and began to spread her arms wide, Christ-like. The spotlight closed in around her, a small girl in a pink sweatshirt and pigtails suspended in space for one last breath before the lights went black. I could barely watch this part of the play, but I did, holding my breath. I was completely still, mesmerized by the action on stage. Internally, though, I was roiling, trying to quell the inexorable surge of anguish and regret for what she'd lost, while also sensing the pride that rose with her voice: powerful and sweet and pure. I wondered, watching her figure balancing in space, if Seth had spread his arms wide in that way, imagining he could fly, for a few moments at least, before plunging down. This was the flip side of my nightmare, that he'd experienced a sense of flight, a slight lift-off toward a simple, soaring childhood dream during his final seconds of consciousness.

Chapter 37

Detours

I would often get stuck on Seth's last moments: Did he jump or fall, soar momentarily or instantly black out? Sometimes, there were no obvious triggers for my morbid ricocheting. It happened even after years had passed, when I believed all that grief-induced vertigo was over. Sometimes the triggers were clear, though, like on a stressful, mad-dash trip to the airport, when I found myself, again unintentionally, heading toward the Tobin Bridge. We were already late, rerouted due to construction. Moungi, driving, turned to me, knowing my bridge-issues, and asked what I wanted to do. There were two options, both bad: Take a detour and likely miss our flight or cross the bridge. "Detour," I said. Then, reconsidering, I thought, maybe now's the time to face it, quickly, with someone else at the wheel. "Fuck it, just cross the bridge," I said. Steeling myself, I began preparing to look over the ledge, relive the final minute, to know exactly how far he fell.

At that moment Moungi waved his phone in the air: the GPS had found another route! I was so relieved, I didn't even care if we took this flight at all.

Long before I met Seth, I knew of the Tobin through its grim notoriety. It was the bridge Charles Stuart jumped from in early January 1990, after murdering his pregnant wife and fabricating a story to police that a young Black kid committed the crime. The Tobin, both aesthetically and historically, had always been tarnished—a symbol of wrongness.

Frankly, I'm not sure its grip will ever release me. In a kind of post-traumatic habit, it's become instinctual for me to compare all other bridges to the Tobin. Visiting my parents in New York, I'd run across the Brooklyn Bridge, which seemed so much friendlier, more survivable. The Sagamore Bridge, which links Cape Cod to the mainland, exudes a sense of purity, functionality, and for me, it's generally a sight for celebration. "We're crossing the bridge," I'd say, phoning my mother or in-laws to let them know we'd be arriving soon. Even the sign at the bridge's entrance—"Desperate, Call the Samaritans"—offered a kind of old-fashioned, rotary-phone-era hope. Just dial this number, help is close at hand.

Whenever the morning news reported a "backup on the Tobin," a prickly heat began to rise up my neck. The Tobin Bridge made me feel as if I could lose my mind. It taunted and dared me to imagine the feel of death. It lured me into Seth's mortal dilemma: I must fight, I can't fight.

On most days, I don't live like this. On most days, I inhabit a far less charged atmosphere, one consumed with the more modest highs and lows of domesticity. I tried to focus on these: a run along the river, a clever plan to juggle kid pickups, the fruit bowl overflowing with summer peaches and plums and the fresh dill growing out back.

These pedestrian moments, it turns out, offer a kind of therapeutic detour, a balm for lurking grief. I learned about this from another researcher, Noam Schneck, at Columbia. I paid him a visit in late summer, a few years after Seth's death, at his research lab in upper Manhattan. Schneck and his graduate students were studying the neurology of grief by examining images of people's brains. They were trying to figure out why some people who lose a loved one to suicide recover, while others suffer from more complex and intractable sorrow that drags on for years, diminishing the survivors' own life. Schneck's research suggests that in addition to the intense emotional distress and preoccupation with loss that characterizes acute grief, there is another, parallel process taking place that actually helps people to heal. Schneck called it "unconscious loss processing" and it occurs outside our awareness. He found that individuals who are more adept at this type of stealth processing tend to experience fewer symptoms of long-term psychic pain and prolonged grief compared to others.

Put another way, while the conscious mind is busy focusing on the humdrum aspects of daily life—shopping, childcare, work—the unconscious machinery keeps chugging away, sifting through loss and working towards a kind of livable acceptance.

Intuitively, I believed in this research because I'd experienced it. Over time, grief became more like background noise, subsumed to daily demands. This didn't happen in a moment; I couldn't see it coming. But at a certain point, I'd crossed a threshold, when the unimaginable—living without Seth—became, simply, life.

Chapter 38

The Last Party

"Should we do the party?"

It would be year four. I'd asked the kids this question as the weather warmed, and we swapped our heavy boots for sandals. I wondered if the fact of our move to Moungi's house eclipsed the very reason for the gathering in the first place: To show that we'd survived, in a kind of belty, Gloria Gaynor style.

I was surprised by the swift response. Sophia immediately asked to invite her friends. Julia dove into recipe research, choosing a mixed berry tart with an old-fashioned lattice design on top, chocolate peanut butter truffles and her veggie quiches with double the ricotta. There was no question that the party would proceed.

The rain had eased to a drizzle as our guests drifted casually in. Some hadn't yet seen our new home. Several of my girlfriends had, by this time, endured their own struggles. We'd held emergency meetings at night to brainstorm strategies after one kid spent a week in the psychiatric ward, when another was caught selling pot at school, when an eating disorder finally came to light. We called ourselves "soul sisters in extreme parenting" and accompanied each other in and out of fear and fragility. I saw that my role had shifted over these years. It felt good to be the mom who could offer comfort in a crisis, rather than the desperate, needy one.

After we all drank plenty of prosecco, I shushed the crowd milling around the kitchen. A few of Seth's colleagues and I had created a new prize to honor his legacy, and I'd been reviewing his research. His students had continued much of the work; the smart wheelchair was already being used at a local senior care unit; the sensor vest to orient blind people and help them navigate the physical world was inching closer to reality.

"Seth always envisioned his work as moving from the impossible to the possible," I said to everyone. "A little like what we've all done together."

This discovery, that we could be happy again, emboldened me. I didn't trust it fully, but recognized it absolutely. Thus energized, I upped the drama for my toast. Moungi and I had been out to see the band Pink Martini a few nights earlier. Mid-concert, the lead singer invited everyone in the audience who identified as female to join her on stage to sing Helen Reddy's "I Am Woman."

Needless to say, I rose to my feet, ran up to a mic, and, recalling most of the lyrics, let loose the '70s anthem. It was supremely cathartic, and I wanted to recreate that moment at our party. I passed out the printed lyrics while my children cringed. "No, Mom, please," they begged. I ignored them. When the adults began to sing, the sound was quiet at first, timid. But soon the volume and power rose, eventually filling the space with a kind of off-key bravado. That's when I realized what these parties had done for us. Together we were evidence that the simple act of holding on—to each other, to ourselves—was meaningful and life-affirming. Seth had died, but in our rough, out-of-tune state, we were okay, more than that, invincible. We attempted harmony as the kids covered their ears.

Then, as I raised a glass to signal the performance had ended, I flashed back to Seth, his luminous smile a beacon in that white jacket on the beach. He would have been 54 that day. Time compressed as I felt all at once the thrill of our first meeting at the airport; that initial glimpse of Sophia, our first child, with her dark curls; Julia standing tall on his shoulders, spring-boarding high in the air before tumbling into the water. So much of our anguish was now tidied up into stories we told our friends, late at night, or over drinks. The kids, too, had learned to harness their own narratives. In sixth grade, Julia was assigned an essay about an important memory: She chose to recount the moment I'd told her Seth had died. My response went from, "Oh, poor Julia," to, "Oy, that poor teacher." And finally, "What courage."

This posthumous party made a statement. It was a deeply considered celebration that emerged from our bottomless need that first year, and evolved into a messy, defiant act: simply slogging through. We'd stumbled, fallen, but now, unwittingly found ourselves upright, on a clear path, emerging from the impossible to the possible.

Moungi stood amidst my friends with a quiet pride, and when I looked over, his eyes caught mine in a way that made my heart skip. His understated ways didn't generally fire up a crowded room, but his face always lit up when I entered a room. "Hey, Beautiful," he'd say, when I tap tap tapped down the stairs in boots and jeans on a weeknight, animated and all set for sushi in the neighborhood, or when I'd stride toward him, out of the ocean, my long hair slicked back, saltwater droplets glimmering on my shoulders. He was attentive and observant and the first time he told me he loved me, he said it in French, so it wasn't obvious, and the layers of meaning lingered in the air, like a whiff of honeysuckle along a quiet road.

Sometimes in the late afternoons, the breeze on my body, I still felt like Moungi and I were having a secret affair. I'd get a flash of sensation, just for an instant, that I'd betrayed the vows Seth and I took years ago. But, more often, I felt, in middle age, we'd beaten the odds. With each languid caress and such pleasure in our midst, I was vital and young, with new promise, a little like I'd saved a life: my own.

The next summer, five years after Seth's death, we don't hold the party.

Instead, we host a wedding.

Chapter 39

Lucky Again
(A Marriage of Deep Summer)

Moungi and I walked down the aisle to Stevie Wonder's "Signed, Sealed, Delivered" as our three girls, bright and beaming in their short, flowery dresses, cheered us on. My brother Paul officiated. "Theirs is not a marriage of early spring," he said, loftily. When I heard this, I began to shake my head, subtly, worried that Paul was heading down a dark road with his speech, toward death and cancer and loss and heaviness. But he ignored me: "Theirs is not a marriage of early spring. It is a marriage of deep summer."

I relaxed. Everyone got it: Moungi and I were not youngsters. This union required careful consideration. We needed super-sized carts for the baggage we'd schlepped around over years. We may have started our relationship shiny and new; my hair silky, eyebrows tweezed, words carefully chosen, but by this time, we were completely exposed, with no secrets—together, we'd compared colonoscopies, negotiated new wills. He took pictures of the angry rash on my ass so I could send them to the doctor.

When it was my turn to speak, I let loose without decorum: "The fact that I'm standing here today, in a white dress, with so many people I love, well, it's a fucking miracle."

Those who understood this best were the ones who had also been to my first wedding, 17 years earlier: my mother, who wore the same fuchsia dress as last time ("But it's okay," she said, "because I'm thinner"); my father, now in a wheelchair pushed by my ever-loyal stepmother, neither of them aware that the countdown to his own death had begun; and Seth's steadfast brothers alongside mine.

My bridal vulgarity got a laugh from some, while others winced. But I didn't care. Moungi said something similar but in a much more appropriate fashion. The girls recited a poem they'd written: "You really are such a great mom. And it's amazing that you are always so CALM!"

I changed into a short, black cocktail dress, and Moungi and I performed the sexy salsa dance we'd practiced. He lifted and twirled me as our guests hooted. We nailed the choreography, swinging our hips in unison to a mashup of the Gaga song "Shallow" and a bachata version of "Stand by Me." The teenagers then cleared the floor and we all danced to Aretha Franklin's "Respect," and "Girls Just Want to Have Fun" and "Born This Way." It was raucous, unpretentious and sweaty.

The next morning, we relaxed in our backyard with the kids and extended family, every table and ledge covered with the peony and wildflower centerpieces we'd brought home.

I surveyed this panorama of abundance—the lazy heat, hints of cinnamon rising from the fresh loaves and scones, the children and their cousins in shorts and tank tops hosing each other down to cool off. My big-hearted cousin Josh, a contractor from Truckee, California, was there, and though I didn't know it then, he'd reconnected with my old friend Rachel at the wedding, thus continuing our pattern of triangular friendships with a romance that seemed pre-destined. My kids couldn't believe it, when we found out. We gossiped about Rachel and Josh, tabulating their chances.

Julia said: "If they get married, Rachel will be family."

Sophia nodded: "She already is."

I marveled at my mother, then 83, flitting and laughing as she served second cups of coffee, hugging everyone. Her pleasure made me smile. Somehow, things had gotten easier with my mother. Maybe because my own hard edges had softened.

When I visited her at the beach these days, we sat in chairs like two old ladies. We talked freely about how good the sun felt and the new plays we wanted to see and what we might order for dinner that night. We walked past other people's children with their plastic shovels and thick layers of sunscreen, and nodded at each other, happy to be briefly unencumbered. We stepped into the salt water, brisk and refreshing. "The best medicine," we agreed. She introduced me with pride to the other women at the bay. "This is my daughter."

Once, when we were out sunbathing, the tide rose quickly, soaking our towels. We spread our bodies out on them anyway. "A pogrom is a pogrom," my mother had said, offering her Jewish bumper sticker version of "Shit Happens." We closed our eyes and the words flowed. She was back together with her boyfriend, sort of; my kids would soon be home from camp. We sighed about world events and she asked about our home renovations. We drove to Mac's on the pier for an early dinner—her Greek salad was topped with salmon, mine with scallops. I drank hard cider, she filled a Dixie cup with water. When we thought no one was looking, we stared at our profiles reflected in glass, evaluating the roundness of our bellies.

My mother would now ask me for advice. We didn't talk about Seth or death or divorce anymore because what would that do, after everything, after all these years? We'd become each other's consolation. Nothing turned out as we'd planned, but in her cottage on top of the hill, we both slept deeply and felt safe. I'd unintentionally adopted her habits, the ones I vowed I never would: eating off my children's plates, chattering unaware of the spinach in my teeth, embellishing the good parts of stories with each retelling. Still, I admired the relationships she'd built with my girls. She'd tell them: "You're beautiful and perfect as you are"—she actually hung up a sign saying so on her bathroom mirror. She'd present them with thrift-shop clothes they loved and I didn't: a blue-and-white checked blouse tied up at the midriff, a flared leather mini-skirt, an oversized sparkly bangle.

The passage of time, the fact that they'd grown into teenagers, had allowed me, finally, to tell my daughters about Seth's note.

We were at his parents' house in Truro when I decided to do it. I prepared myself by taking a long run, hugging the shady side of the road, near the field of fiddleheads. As I approached the beach, the smell of wild roses and salt were so familiar, and the heat drew me down to the Bay. I dove into the cool water, reliably curative, and it triggered in me a sense of him, a burst of strength in my limbs as I stroked against the current. Underwater, enmeshed in nature, I was surrounded by forces I knew I couldn't control, and, so, began to let go of control altogether.

Sophia was in high school now, Julia close behind. Since Seth had been gone, they'd taken shape, gained perspective, developed an understanding that the world is complex, and sometimes bad things happen to good people. It suddenly seemed stingy to withhold key information.

I decided that all three of us could handle whatever anger or sadness the note might provoke, so when I got back, I changed into dry clothes and sat in a chair to face them. Then, I blurted it out. "Guys, there's something I haven't mentioned about Dad." They both looked up, concerned.

"He left a note. It says that he loved you, loved us. I didn't tell you earlier because it was so painful to me, and hard, and I didn't know how to explain it to you."

Sophia, in a display of solidarity that surprised me, said: "It's okay, we were so young."

Julia, the ethicist, said: "You should have told us sooner."

"You're right, I should have," I said. "I'm sorry."

Again, Sophia's sympathy struck me: "It's understandable."

I continued: "The note just says his tinnitus got worse and he couldn't make it stop and the last thing he said is that he loves us. He wrote down all our names."

They told me they would read it when they were ready. At home.

Then the moment passed, and we each emerged from its depth in our own manner. The girls started a movie, focused on the small screen blather rather than this big, new fact of their lives.

I stepped outside, drawn to a spot atop the sand dune that grew taller each summer, further hiding the house from the beachgoers below. I sat cross-legged and looked out at the sea, choppy that day with a storm heading up the coast. My belly tightened, giving rise to big, breathy sobs.

It's done, I'd thought, as if the note itself had been surgically removed from my body.

This unburdening of despair, the relinquishing of its weight, put me into such a state of repose, I experienced the lift of freedom. Like the end of a long labor, when the vertiginous, burning pain shifts from relentless to zero at the instant of birth, this sharing of Seth's last words immediately stopped the bone-deep ache I'd clung to, for what purpose, I couldn't even recall.

Suddenly, everything had seemed simpler. There was only the warm sand on my skin, the cool wind, and my eyes fixed on the waves that had held everyone I'd loved. In the crash of surf, I heard words beyond anything on a page: *We are here. We are here. We are here.*

My attention then swiveled back to the jubilant scene playing out in our backyard. Julia approached me with a fresh strawberry, placing it on my tongue. "You've *got* to taste this," she said. "It's super sweet."

If this was the "good life," I thought as we replayed moments from the wedding—the dance, the toasts, the teenagers—perhaps it was born of "a good suicide." Not good, of course, in the act or the pain—never that—but good because we were still standing, making plans for the afternoon, the next day and years beyond, embracing the idea of a future.

There was good merely in the girls' growing up. They'd become powerful and opinionated, arguing about justice and the imperiled climate; they were in love with their friends, cried openly when they were hurt. They held memories intact: "You Are My Sunshine," leaf jumping, his favorite apple cake, and they transformed those memories into art and stories of their own.

And just as we settled into one story, it changed, and we did too. So, at this wedding I could quote Thoreau without irony—"There is no remedy for love but to love more"—and believe, even now, with sorrow we can't erase, images we still won't face, we are, in the end, lucky.

EPILOGUE

The Good in What Remains

Five years after my husband's suicide, I am folding his laundry. From a large basket, I pull out the soft, black and white T-shirts he wore to play Ultimate on Tuesday nights. His shorts are here too: Each pair the same, loose cotton that hung low on his hips, nearly a dozen in various earth tones. If they came from a stylish catalog they'd be marketed as sandstone, red-rock, brushed camel. But Seth wasn't fancy; he'd call them yellow, red, brown. I examine his socks, a sad collection of faded white anklets and tubes from Target. They are threadbare.

I hadn't thought much about the clothes Maria had packed into garbage bags, banished to the basement just days after his death. But now, in early summer, Sophia asks to visit the old house. She explains that she wants to have dinner with Maria, who's still living there, and to sleep in her childhood room, the one she'd decorated with self-portraits and family trees, and, later, pictures of Seth to stir her memory.

My first impulse is to say "no." I want to protect her from the house, which, to me, remains frozen in time, haunted, chaotic. We'd moved out haphazardly, as if we were just taking a short trip, not turning our backs on a life that was upended when the girls were little. We only took what we needed, and, like harried evacuees rushing to beat an impending storm, left the rest. In the years since his death, I'd never properly sorted through the things Seth loved and left. On the bookshelves in his office, the hard-cover collections of classic comics—*Ignatz and Krazy Kat*, Art Spiegelman's *Maus* series, all the *Peanuts* strips—remained in place; downstairs cubbies overflowed with jigsaw puzzles, his Ph.D. thesis, Slinkies and stilts unused for years.

But my impulsive "no" melts into an emphatic, "Yes, of course you can visit." *This was healthy,* I thought, *resilience in action, my daughter's way of keeping that portion of her life intact.* "Go, sleep in your bed, you should do it," I say. Soon, though, I grasp the other reason—perhaps the real reason—she is keen on the visit: his clothes. To her, these items are not markers of death. They're a fashion statement. She's eager to thrift amidst this treasure trove.

Sophia spends several hours in the damp basement, ripping open garbage bags, sorting through piles. Afterwards, she calls me, elated. "Such cool shirts," she says, "and some jeans. I can make them work, I'll show you."

Several weeks later, when Julia returns from sleepaway camp and hears about her sister's vintage clothing excursion, she wants a piece of the action. "When can I go?" she begs, as if she doesn't already have a lifetime of hand-me-down jeans and colorful crop tops. Still, with two daughters, the illusion of parity is vital for peacekeeping.

I drive Julia to the old house and she heads straight to the basement. It's dank from the previous day's downpour, but she doesn't notice. She spots the torn-open garbage bags and digs in with both hands. Julia has always been methodical. Here, she carefully unfolds each T-shirt, each pair of shorts, and deploys a measured, analytical evaluation of every item. Her sorting process takes into account many factors: emotional valence, memories evoked, coolness, and the sheer desire to match and surpass her sister's loot.

Of course, she wants the *Amazing Spider Man* tees, and the one featuring Milou, the wire fox terrier from *Tintin*. But she also goes for the entire bag of socks. I see no hip factor in these socks, nor the many Boston Ultimate Disc Association shirts from the '90s tagged with random phrases ("Wake Up and Smell the Frisbee") and myriad tech conference giveaways. I sit on the splintery basement steps fighting my own sense of remorse. A stain of injustice still marks this house, these objects—Why him? Why us? It takes some effort to breathe down here: the air is thick, stale. As I observe Julia assessing each piece of clothing, a familiar tinge of vertigo sets in.

She and I don't speak much. As she holds up a shirt, I tilt my head and imagine our simultaneous memory of his muscular arms covered in dark hair—the girls called it fur when they were small—emerging from the now-lifeless sleeves. She wraps a pair of shorts around her waist and confidently swishes her hips, and the movement rekindles his playfulness, the way he'd dance around after finding a lost object. I can see that my daughter finds deep comfort in these clothes, an actual piece of him returned. Satisfied, she carefully refolds each shirt and pair of shorts and places them in the "keep" pile. She keeps pretty much everything.

I want to get out. I'm dizzy and begin to feel the burden of these clothes, all the extra washing and folding, more chores tacked on to an endless to-do list. But I know that the true cause of my unease is the psychic weight of his laundry, resurrected. Outside of this basement I've "moved on," set up house with a good and grounded man in a brighter space, with a dry basement and an abundant garden I can walk through barefoot, snipping rosemary and parsley, plucking sweet cherry tomatoes off the vine. Down here I face stagnation, ghosts, a partner pledged to me but no longer mine.

Seth wore the same clothes, these clothes, every day. Now I see clearly, maybe for the first time, that his body is no longer in them. There will be no more Saturday mornings, sneaking back to bed, the kids downstairs glued to a movie and sated by a simple bowl of warm, sweet oats. No more holding hands on the beach planning the next birthday party or wondering what we'd grill for supper that night. The deep mourning for the life we'd built had been sealed up, dormant, like an old coat of lead paint that's stable, until a child chips away a layer, exposing its toxicity. *Seth is dead,* these clothes whisper, *gone.*

It's different for Julia, I see that. Indeed, when I finally pry myself loose from personal pity, two thoughts come to me at the same time: *Why didn't I throw this crap out?* And, *How wonderful that I didn't.*

"All set," Julia says. We heave four, full 30-gallon trash bags up the stairs and into the car. At home, the girls trade and compare items like it's Halloween and they're negotiating Charleston Chews and Kit Kats. When they begin pulling shirts over their heads, I stop them: everything's got to be washed.

There are so many clothes that we all take a basket, and the ritual of washing and folding and storing spans days and then weeks. Gradually, the clothes insinuate themselves into the daily rotation, sometimes as nightgowns, billowing down to their knees, or as statements—"2 Nice Girls"—or they'll pair his faded shorts with a paisley tube top. Soon I notice even more of him hanging around: the nylon sports pants he threw on when shoveling snow from our front yard while the children sipped cocoa; the jacket he always wore when he took the girls to visit Atlas, the robot. All of Seth's clothes are roomy and comfortable and I begin to think that they formed a deliberate costume, a casual exterior that was the precise inverse of the tightening grip inside his brain.

On the first day of school that year, Julia, a gymnast now, strong and compact and muscular like Seth, wears his Krazy Kat shirt. When he died, she was a petite pixie scrambling up to the top of the monkey bars. Now she's checking Instagram and lecturing me about gender politics.

I wave goodbye as she skips off with a friend, buzzing and excited for the day. The cold air has set in and the transition to fall, so destabilizing for the past five years, seems particularly harsh now. September was when we got married, when the promise of home and family seemed so certain. September was also when I fully explained the word "suicide" to my children. When they had to answer questions from classmates—

"Where's your dad?"—when we found ourselves in a strange new world, violently altered.

It's late morning, the house is empty. The wind has picked up and I search my drawers for socks, a pair, not the many useless singlets confronting me. I need to run, to shake off the residue of his death, which still surges, now and then, without warning. I enter my daughter's room and rummage around: Seth's socks lay in a heap. I find a pair and, on examination, see that they've lost their elasticity; there's a small hole near the heel. I could toss them away and no one would notice.

Instead, I sit on the floor and slide the socks over my toes, still brown from the summer sun. I wiggle them around, enjoying the unexpected roominess, and slip on my old sneakers. Then I rise to my feet, head outside and toward the river. Settling into a comfortable stride, I imagine Seth cushioning each step like a sheath, a memory of shelter; a thin veneer that remains.

Acknowledgements

This book has been a 10-year effort, one that would have been impossible for me to complete on my own. I was fortunate to be able to lean on a generous, talented writing community, in particular, my teacher and mentor, Alysia Abbott, as well as trusted readers and writing comrades, Doug Smith, Patty Caya, Aimee Seiff Christian, Ananda Lowe, Karen Weintraub, Katie Leisener, Annie Brewster, Miriam Glassman, Sue Shepard, Jean Lenihan, Becky Tuch, Michelle Bowdler, Sandra Miller, Maya Shanbhag Lang, Kristen Paulsen-Nguyen, Nell Lake, Lara Wilson, and affiliates of Grub Street's Memoir Incubator program. For providing me with the time and space to write, thanks to administrators of the Turkey Land Cove Foundation and Millay Arts residencies. The team at Santa Fe Writers Project, notably the gifted editor Adam al-Sirgany, made the book stronger.

Some material in *Us, After* has been previously published, including in *O, The Oprah Magazine*, November 2020; *The Cut*, August 2018; and vogue.com, May 2018. Thanks to Allan Ko for allowing me to quote from his thesis, "The Cultural Life of Suicide: Observing Care and Death at MIT."

Friends and family took care of my daughters and me all along the way. Deep love and appreciation to my amazing mother, Selma; as well as my brothers, Paul and Nick; stepmother, Betsy; Seth's parents, Sam and Joan; his brothers and their wives, Adam and Cathy and David and Jil; and the extended Teller family. Also, many thanks to my stepdaughter, Mia, for her love and acceptance. I am grateful to Maria for all those hours and days. My father did not survive to see this book make it into the world, but he lives in these pages. My girlfriends literally saved me, among them, Sarah, Tal, both Amy's, Rachel, Natasha, Hillary, Pam, Jean, Kira, Karen, Anne, Carey, Kirsten, Tanya, Sue, Melissa, Dune, Penelope, Meg, Lizzie, Alyssa, and Ann. My exquisite partner, Moungi Bawendi, kept me going with love, patience, and sustenance.

This book is dedicated to Seth, with love, always. And especially, to my wise and beautiful daughters, Sophia and Julia, who delight and inspire me every day; you are the heroes of the story, and this is a love letter to you.

About the Author

Rachel Zimmerman, an award-winning journalist, has written about health and medicine for more than two decades. She's a contributor to *The Washington Post*, and previously worked as a staff writer for *The Wall Street Journal* and a health reporter for WBUR, Boston's public radio station, where she co-founded a popular blog and podcast. Her essays and reporting have been published in *The New York Times*; *Vogue.com*; New York Magazine's *The Cut*; *O, The Oprah Magazine*; *The Atlantic*; *Slate*; and *The Huffington Post*, among others. She is co-author of *The Healing Power of Storytelling* (North Atlantic Books, 2020) and *The Doula Guide to Birth* (Bantam/Random House, 2009). Zimmerman has been awarded residencies at Millay Arts and the Turkey Land Cove Foundation. She received an MS from Columbia University Graduate School of Journalism and a BA from Sarah Lawrence College. She lives with her family in Cambridge, Mass. Find her at rachelzimmerman.net.

Also from Santa Fe Writers Project

About Santa Fe Writers Project

SFWP is an independent press founded in 1998 that embraces a mission of artistic preservation, recognizing exciting new authors, and bringing out of print work back to the shelves.

 @santafewritersproject | X @SFWP | sfwp.com sfwp)